"The one thing we have dominion over in our life is our thoughts, but so many of us are trapped in habitual or worrisome thinking that is not creating the results we desire in life. With cutting-edge techniques, *Think Forward to Thrive* empowers us to think in a way that not only supports our well-being in the moment but also creates a desirable future."

— Christine Hassler, author of *Expectation Hangover* and
20 Something, 20 Everything

"You hold in your hands a wonderful vehicle for getting unstuck from the ruts of depression, anxiety, and hopelessness. Jennice Vilhauer skillfully blends inspiring, anecdotal stories with evidence-based skills and tools designed to help anyone participate more fully in her or his life. If you've ever wanted to be more in control of where your emotions, thoughts, beliefs, and actions were leading you, *Think Forward to Thrive* can give you the kind of positive traction necessary to move forward — and toward a more fulfilling and transformative life journey. Highly recommended!"

— Donald Altman, MA, LPC, author of
The Mindfulness Toolbox and *One-Minute Mindfulness*

"If you feel stuck or find yourself struggling to meet your goals, this may be the most important book you will ever buy. Basing her work on current neuroscience research, Jennice Vilhauer has created an accessible guide for breaking free of the past and learning to live the life you want."

— Marissa Burgoyne, PsyD, psychologist, Pepperdine University and UCLA

FUTURE DIRECTED THERAPY®

THINK FORWARD
TO
THRIVE

FUTURE DIRECTED THERAPY®

THINK FORWARD
TO
THRIVE

HOW TO USE THE MIND'S POWER
OF ANTICIPATION TO TRANSCEND
YOUR PAST AND TRANSFORM YOUR LIFE

Jennice Vilhauer, PhD

New World Library
Novato, California

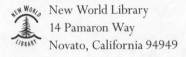 New World Library
14 Pamaron Way
Novato, California 94949

Text design by David Moratto

Library of Congress Cataloging-in-Publication Data
Vilhauer, Jennice.
Think forward to thrive : how to use the mind's power of anticipation to transcend your past and transform your life / Jennice Vilhauer.
    pages   cm
Includes bibliographical references and index.
ISBN 978-1-60868-298-0 (paperback) — ISBN 978-1-60868-299-7 (ebook)
1. Self-actualization (Psychology). I. Title.
BF637.S4.V55 2014
158.1—dc23   2014013793

First printing, October 2014
ISBN 978-1-60868-298-0
Printed in Canada on 100% postconsumer-waste recycled paper

 New World Library is proud to be a Gold Certified Environmentally Responsible Publisher. Publisher certification awarded by Green Press Initiative. www.greenpressinitiative.org

10 9 8 7 6 5 4 3 2 1

To my patients and my students,
who always inspire me — this is for you.

The future belongs to those who believe in the beauty of their dreams.
—ELEANOR ROOSEVELT

CONTENTS

An Introduction to

FUTURE DIRECTED THERAPY

*It is far more important for man to know
whom he wants to become than who he is now.*
— JOSEPH NUTTIN

Everyone wants to feel good, everyone wants to thrive, yet many people don't
know how to make this happen. **Future Directed Therapy (FDT)** is a
whole new approach to improving how we function, based on the idea that
because we can only move forward in time, we can only fully be understood as beings continuously in the process of becoming. The "future" in Future Directed
Therapy is not necessarily far off in time; it can refer to any point in time beyond
the present moment, near or far. Rather, FDT is about understanding that because
we can only move forward, most of our thinking and behavior is anticipatory or
future oriented. We constantly speculate about *what will happen*, whether in the
very next moment, tomorrow, or five years from now, and that has a huge impact
on how we process information, how we feel about different situations, how we
interact with our environment, and ultimately how we create our lives.

Although we often think the past dictates our behavior, the *future* is what really
motivates most of our actions. Whether you are motivated to go to the kitchen
because you anticipate eating something delicious, or you are motivated to save
money because you want to buy a new home, or you are motivated to take any other
action you could possibly imagine, you *act* because you *expect* a certain desired
result. The past is relevant only to the extent that we use it to *predict* the future.

A primary premise of Future Directed Therapy is that what people *want* (any
desired future state) is the fundamental motivating force behind their behavior.
Often we act to avoid something undesirable, but it is our desire to avoid the
unwanted that drives our behavior. For example, if you decide not to go to an
anxiety-provoking party, it is because you *want* to avoid an uncomfortable situation.
Because we believe that the things we want will bring about some desired future
state, when we focus our thinking on what we want, we experience positive emotions. When you think about having a positive experience in the future or getting

something you want, you feel great; when you think about taking actions to avoid an uncomfortable situation, you feel relief.

However, when we focus on what we don't want, we experience emotional distress and suffering. If instead you think about missing out on an opportunity to see your friends or disappointing the person who invited you to the party, you may feel guilt or sadness. We can have thoughts about both the wanted *and* the unwanted aspects of any situation. If you want to lose weight, you can think about how great it will feel when you do (wanted) or how lousy it is to give up your favorite foods (unwanted). Our minds tend to jump between wanted and unwanted situations all day long without our ever even realizing it is happening.

The key to thriving is learning to harness the mind's natural tendency to antic-ipate the future so that you can focus most of your attention on what you would like to achieve. This not only brings you positive emotions, but it also activates a series of mental functions that actually increase your ability to obtain what you desire. Whenever you think about your desired future state, several solution-generating, problem-solving mechanisms in your brain kick into gear. However, when you focus on what you don't want and you experience the resulting negative emotions, this inhibits the area of your brain responsible for these functions from working properly.[1] The longer you think about what you want, the harder these mechanisms work, often leading to ideas and solutions that never would have occurred to you if you had not focused on your desired future.

Think Forward to Thrive is a step-by-step guide to learning how to experience more positive emotions and to thrive more by focusing on what you want; it will teach you the skills you need to begin creating your future by choice. While FDT comes from the field of psychology, it is far more than just a form of therapy. It is a way to live that maximizes the full potential of all human beings to create the experiences they want.

THE LIGHT AT THE END OF THE TUNNEL

My idea for FDT came from years of working as a psychologist, listening to people talk about their pasts but rarely seeing them make significant life changes. I felt a deep sense of guilt and frustration because I felt what I had to offer to my patients wasn't enough. I had been trained to believe that understanding one's past and working through unresolved conflicts was the key to feeling better. My desire to help my patients make more rapid changes and develop better ways to cope with their difficult circumstances led me to the world of cognitive behav-ioral therapy, in which I learned that people could make changes by modifying their thoughts and behaviors in the present moment. While I found cognitive ther-apy to be substantially more practical and tangible for my clients, it still left many unanswered questions about what motivated change, and clients often found that labeling their thinking as irrational, one of the common tools of cognitive therapy, seemed to invalidate their experiences.

One day I was listening to a particularly depressed client, whom I had been seeing for about six months, once again tell me about his daunting life circumstances. In the time we had worked together, he had made little progress shifting his negative thinking on these issues. I asked him from a place of both frustration and pure instinct, "So where is the light at the end of the tunnel?" He looked at me with a completely blank expression and then admitted that there wasn't one. "Well, no wonder you are depressed," I said. "Your life is awful, and you can't see any way it is going to get better."

"But I don't know how to change my life," he replied.

"Well, from now on, the focus of our work together is going to be creating that light at the end of the tunnel."

One year later, my client had radically transformed his life. He had gone from working in a dead-end job that he hated to owning a successful business, something he had never dared to dream of before.

After that session, I began to ask all my clients about their light at the end of the tunnel. I was startled to realize that most of them didn't feel they had one. Either they felt that life would never change, or they worried it would only get worse. Most of them didn't know how to change their future, and many of them didn't even believe it was possible. As my work with clients began to focus almost exclusively on helping them to create better pictures of their futures, I noticed without exception that those who were able not only to develop a more positive outlook on their future but also to take action began to feel better. The transformations I saw people making were awe-inspiring.

At the same time, wanting to help my clients develop better skills for creating their futures, I began to search the psychology literature for information on future thinking. I discovered a body of scientific work that had yet to be translated into any type of practical intervention — work providing valid support for the idea that anticipating a positive future and feeling able to act on that future were the keys to emotional well-being. I knew the challenge to translate this information into something useful would be daunting, but I kept my focus on what I wanted, which was to get this information into the hands of my clients. It is to my clients with whom I have had the privilege of working that I dedicate this book.

THE BASICS OF FDT

A fundamental premise of Future Directed Therapy is that all human beings desire to thrive. In FDT thriving is defined as a dynamic state of growth and of moving forward toward improved life circumstances from wherever one is in the present. Everyone wants to thrive, though everyone has a different idea of what thriving is, based on his or her circumstances. For some people, thriving might be the opportunity to eat regular meals; for some, it might be buying a yacht; for others, it might be attaining spiritual enlightenment. Thriving is about constantly *feeling* you can grow, move forward, and improve your life circumstances.

It is well documented that no matter what we achieve, we are never satisfied for very long.[2] While many explanations of this phenomenon have been offered, such as the idea that our ability to experience happiness is limited or that discontent is a moral deficiency, in FDT the constant desire to thrive and move forward is viewed as a psychological drive with a biological basis. New technological advances allowing us to study brain functioning have revealed the critical role that the area of the brain responsible for *reward processing* plays in our daily lives. Rewards are the things we look forward to in the future; they are essential to our emotional well-being. The absence of rewards leads to negative emotions, which is why the onset of many psychiatric conditions is often linked to the loss of the things people find rewarding, such as relationships or jobs.[3] Unfortunately, people with a wide variety of emotional problems experience impairments in their brains' ability to identify or process rewards.[4] This may explain why, even when someone has many positive things in his life, when he is feeling down he finds it much easier to focus on the negative. Someone with an impaired reward system might have a great job but only focus on the long commute there, or easily recall a critical comment about a work project, but seem unable to hear the twenty compliments that were also given.

When the brain's reward-processing system doesn't operate properly, not only do people become depressed, but they also lose the desire to pursue what they want.[5] Even activities that may have felt exciting and rewarding before, such as going to a concert or a movie, seem like too much effort. This is because when certain neurotransmitters in the brain's reward-processing center, particularly dopamine, are low, this condition can lead us to overestimate the costs associated with pursuing things that would be rewarding, making the depressed person feel as if it isn't worth exerting the effort to obtain something wanted.[6] Not surprisingly, when the reward center in a person's brain is underactive, he ends up participating in fewer activities that would provide stimulation to this brain region.[7] Going to the concert or the movie, whether or not he felt like it, would activate this part of the brain, and he would feel better.

One hypothesis in FDT is that the desire to pursue rewards and to thrive promotes the evolutionary progression of humankind. Every human invention, from the first stone tool to the supercomputers we use today, has been driven by the desire to improve our circumstances. In order for forward movement and thriving to continue, there must always be a difference between where we are in life and where we want to be. In FDT we believe that our desire to close this gap creates what is referred to as the *need to want*. Humans need to want things in order to keep moving forward. And what we want is always in the future.

We cannot move forward without exerting a want, intent, or desire. If you finish reading this page, it is because you want to do so. Each time we realize a future-oriented desire, a new desire emerges. When you finish reading this page, you will want to keep reading more, or you will want to put the book down and go do something else. Every action is a choice that requires intent or desire in order for it to manifest as a physical experience. In FDT we believe that when people feel they have the power to obtain what they want, they experience well-being. However, when they feel they are unable to move into their desired future state, they experience distress. If you decided you wanted to go for a walk and buy ice cream, and someone told you that you had no choice but to sit in a chair and read this book until the very end, whether or not you wanted to, you would probably find this upsetting (even though it is a really good book!).

We use a creative thought process to generate ideas about what we want, develop plans to obtain what we want, and initiate the actions needed to make our plans become reality. If you decide you want ice cream, for example, your brain immediately starts to think of ways to make this occur — you think about where to buy the ice cream, what kind you want to buy, and so forth. This process leads to planning and problem solving that increase your likelihood of realizing your desire.

In FDT we believe that people experience emotional suffering when they spend too much time thinking about what they do not want. Pretty much anything you can think of that makes you feel bad is something you don't want. *I don't want my car to break down, I don't want my husband to leave me, I don't want to lose my job, I don't want my parents to die.*

It gets a bit more complex when at first you start to think about what you do want, but then you shift your focus to something you don't want on the same subject. If you decide you want ice cream because it is hot outside and it sounds like a refreshing treat but then start thinking about the ice cream making you fat, which is an outcome you don't want, instead of feeling good about the ice cream, you will start to feel anxious.

It is important to recognize that when you have a desire but don't yet have what you want, this is an unwanted state. For example, if you want a relationship but don't have one, not having one is something unwanted. Often people think they are focusing on what they want, but if they are not feeling good about it, what they are likely focusing on is the fact that they do not yet have what they want. *I really want to be more organized but my house is such a mess; I get overwhelmed thinking about it.* They may draw conclusions that what they want makes them anxious so they try not to think about it. But this is never the case. Negative emotions are always the result of giving attention to some unwanted aspect of a situation.

FDT teaches people to recognize that their emotions are indicators of what they've been thinking about. In other words, if you are experiencing a positive emotion such as gratitude or contentment, you are focused on the wanted aspect of a subject, but if you are feeling a negative emotion such as anger or fear, it is because you are thinking about something in your life that you do not want. It is specifically this focus on the unwanted thing or situation that moves you away from a state of thriving and leads to emotional distress. If you think long enough about what you do not want in your life, you may become depressed or anxious. In FDT people are taught to observe their feelings and to shift the focus of their thinking toward more of what they want in life.

To put it simply, FDT is about helping people to identify the process by which they create their future and to direct the process in a way that generates a greater sense of thriving and well-being. In this book you will learn how your thoughts about the future are often based on existing limiting belief systems and how to create new, more positive expectations about what the future holds. You will also learn how to better allocate your valuable resources, such as thought, behavior, and time, toward obtaining more of what you desire, by clarifying and prioritizing your wants based on what you value.

Another important skill you will learn is to define realistic goals and also to deal more effectively with the aspects of a situation that are beyond your control. An important concept in FDT is the idea that humans grow and expand through experience, and you will learn to use those times when you do not get what you want as opportunities for growth and self-awareness.

Many of the techniques outlined in these pages are based on what psychologists refer to as a "neurobehavioral approach," which looks at how your brain and your behavior work together.[8] A good deal of research has shown that you can activate parts of your brain at will, with your attention and behavior.[9] While this can be challenging at first, over time you can learn to change your brain's structures and the way it functions.[10] The brain is a lot like a sophisticated computer — it can do wonderful things if you know how to use it, but if you don't, you both miss out on its benefits and become quite frustrated. Once you know how your brain works, you can make it work for *you*. Many of the practice exercises in this book will help you learn the skills to purposefully generate the mental activity, and eventually the behaviors, that can turn what you want into an experience you actually live.

MARY'S STORY

Mary was a thirty-one-year-old singer-songwriter struggling with depression and anxiety. She had recently moved from Canada to Los Angeles with her boyfriend of almost four years so that he could pursue his interest in screenwriting and she could pursue her singing career. By most musicians' standards, Mary had already experienced a fair amount of success. Several years earlier she had been signed to a major record label and produced an album, but because the album wasn't promoted well, the sales hadn't been high and the label had chosen not to renew her contract. Even though Mary had been singing since she was a child, she no longer got any pleasure from working on her music, and she was feeling at a loss over what to do with her life. Mary was supporting herself by waiting tables in a small restaurant, a job that she found very unsatisfying, given that she had a bachelor's degree in art history from a top college.

In addition to feeling unhappy with her professional life, Mary was also unhappy with her personal life. She hadn't made any new friends since her move, and she felt that her life outside work was empty. She didn't want to talk to new people because she feared they would see her as a failure. She was also frustrated with her boyfriend, who she had lived with for more than three years, because he had not yet proposed; she felt that he avoided the subject of marriage. Mary did not have much of a relationship with her family, either. She felt her parents were disappointed in her because they had worked hard to put her through college and she wasn't working in a "real" job. Her fear of disapproval and criticism often made her irritable, and she could be short-tempered with her parents, which made her feel guilty, so she often avoided talking to them.

Mary spent a good deal of her day thinking about all the unhappy areas of her life. She had very little energy and had difficulty getting out of bed because she dreaded facing each day. When she opened her eyes in the morning, she would start to list all the things in her life that made her unhappy. She felt like a failure at music and believed that maybe it was time to give in to her family's pressure to get a real job, but she didn't know what other kind of career to pursue because nothing felt interesting to her. She also worried that, because of her depression, her boyfriend would leave her and she would be completely alone. She felt trapped and unmotivated, and she had a hard time seeing any way for things to improve.

Mary's first task was to learn about her thought process so that she could understand how her thinking was keeping her feeling stuck and unhappy. She learned first to understand that her thinking was a valuable resource that contributed directly to the life she was creating. Also, by paying attention to her emotions, she learned to identify how she was using this resource. She learned that, when she was feeling bad, it was a direct result of her focusing her thoughts on the areas of her life in which she was unhappy, and she learned to recognize that as long as she kept doing so, she would not generate any new ideas about how to realize her desires. She then learned the skill of redirecting her thoughts. She created a list of things that she could focus on to generate positive feelings, and she kept the list with her so that she could pull it out when she needed it. The list reminded her of all the wanted aspects of her life and would take her thoughts in a better direction whenever she started a downward spiral. This allowed her to improve her mood and regain some perspective.

Next, Mary learned to understand how her thinking was directly affecting her choices. She saw that she was creating negative future projections based on past experiences, then engaging in behavior consistent with what she was expecting, thereby creating self-fulfilling prophecies. She was able to see that she was fearful of failing at her music career because her first album had been unsuccessful; therefore, she wasn't putting any effort into her career, guaranteeing future failure. She also learned that, because she feared criticism and rejection, she was withdrawing and acting in a way that was making her boyfriend and her family more likely to criticize and reject her.

Mary learned to use what she didn't want to help her identify what she did want, and she learned that when she focused on what she did want, her mind would generate ideas and solutions to help her achieve her goals. Every time she had a thought about something she didn't want, she didn't allow her thinking to stop there, as she had in the past. When she felt the communication with her boyfriend wasn't going well, instead of staying focused on the lack of communication and how bad it made her feel, she reminded herself that what she really wanted in the situation was to communicate effectively with him, and she tried to think of ways to make this happen. She made a conscious effort to start telling her boyfriend what she liked about him and their relationship, and tried focusing discussions on ways to improve the relationship as opposed to always complaining about what was making her unhappy.

When Mary was able to identify what she wanted, she started to develop concrete goals for herself and learned how to create new expectations that brought her closer to where she wanted to be. Instead of believing that because her music career had not been as successful as she wanted in the past it was doomed to failure in the future, she chose to create a new future expectation by initiating the new thought that *she could succeed if she tried hard enough*. She worked to grow this new thought about her future into a belief by taking as many actions as she could that were consistent with the new thought. She also used many techniques and strategies, such as having a conversation with herself as a successful singer, which made her future goal seem more tangible. When she ran into obstacles — such as not having enough money — to her new goal of producing her own album on an independent label, instead of focusing on the problem she didn't want, she maintained a successful mind-set and immediately began generating the solutions she did want. Mary learned to embrace each obstacle as an opportunity to grow, and within six months she had found funding for her new album, hired a music engineer and a designer for her new website, and produced two new songs. She was well on her way to creating the future she wanted.

As Mary began to feel more empowered and more hopeful about her future, her depression subsided rapidly. She looked forward to getting out of bed in the morning because she was focused on creating the things she desired. As a result, every area of her life began to improve, and she began to thrive.

How to Use This Book

Think Forward to Thrive is like an instruction manual for the life you've always wanted. It is packed with information, and all of it will empower you to move forward. However, don't try to read it or do it all at once. The skills in this book are based on established psychological principles combined with cutting-edge research from various fields that study the human mind; they were developed over several years by working with many real people in ten-week courses. Many of the concepts will be new to you, and it is best if you learn them slowly so that you can really absorb and remember the material.

The book is divided into twelve skill-building chapters. While each chapter can stand alone, the chapters are presented in an intentional sequence, so I encourage you to work through the chapters in order. The chapters include practice assignments and worksheets intended to enhance your learning process. You will get the most out of this book if you read one chapter a week while spending at least twenty minutes every day doing the assignments. For your convenience, full-size worksheets are also available for download at www.FutureDirectedTherapy.com; use the first four digits of the ISBN code on the back of this book as the access code.

The "Ask Yourself" questions following the key concepts will help you build an internal dialogue that will bring about deeper self-awareness. You can reflect on these questions and use them daily when you encounter stressful situations or negative emotions. In this way, you'll remind yourself of the process as it occurs and also reinforce the skills you can use to direct the process in a way that moves you closer to what you want.

You are now ready to start developing the skills you need to start creating the life you want. As much as you may want immediate change, don't try to rush the process. It is a journey, and there is much to learn between where you are and where you want to be. Stay the course, and success will be yours.

Clinical Professionals: I look forward to supporting your interest and work with Future Directed Therapy; please see the Letter to Professionals at the end of the book. There are also training materials and other resources available for you at www.futuredirectedtherapy.com.

Chapter 1

A New Beginning

Live out of your imagination, not your history.
— Stephen R. Covey

Imagine that you're traveling through life in a car and you are the driver. Many people are unclear about the direction they are heading in, and some get through life never even learning how to drive. They operate their car in a default mode that allows them to zigzag through life with very little control. Many people get stuck and stalled, while others hit dead ends or go in circles, feeling like they never get anywhere. The goals of Future Directed Therapy (FDT) are to teach you how to drive the car, give you a proper road map to help you reach your destination and, most important, help you stay on course.

The Road to Well-Being

What many people don't realize is that in the journey of life we can head in only two directions: toward well-being and away from it. Your thoughts and actions power your car. Your emotions indicate where you are going. If you are feeling bad, it means you're thinking thoughts that are taking you away from well-being and moving you toward distress. Because we don't control time, and our life keeps progressing, you never completely stand still. You are always moving, whether it be toward thriving or away from it. Allowing a negative stream of thoughts to flow through your mind does not just prevent you from moving toward what you want; it takes you further away from it. The longer you let your thoughts carry you in that direction, the further away you get from your goals and desires.

By the time you are feeling painful emotions, such as anxiety or depression, your thoughts have been flowing as though your car were going a hundred miles an hour — headed in the wrong direction. You can't just shift into reverse when you are going that fast. You need to slow the car down until you are ready to turn it around. The same thing is true of your thought process. By using FDT you will learn how to turn yourself around by redirecting your thinking and reaching for incremental improvements in thought rather than by trying to make fast accelerations that often lead to a crash and burn or, at the very least, get you no closer to your desired destination.

While all human beings are constantly creating their futures, many are not aware of how the process actually occurs, and as a result, they have limited control over what they experience. The process of learning to create your future by choice instead of by default starts with gaining awareness of your thought process and then developing the skills that will help you choose the life you want.

RE-CREATING THE PAST

Most people create their future by re-creating the past. The ability to re-create the past stems from a valuable survival instinct. If we find a good source of food or a safe place to sleep, we want to be able to find it again. If we have a pleasant encounter with someone, we want to have a similar experience again. Our memory is what gives us the ability to store information about our past and present experiences. We use this stored information to formulate expectations about our environment and to make predictions about our future experiences. Being able to predict or anticipate the future enables us to prepare for it by taking the actions we think are necessary to meet future events with success.

For example, if you have been lucky enough to go through life having mostly positive experiences with other people, such as loving parents, lots of friends, great teachers, and nice bosses, you most likely enjoyed these experiences. Because you have had so many positive past experiences, you probably have developed the expectation that most people you meet in the future will treat you well. If you expect people to treat you well, you will likely act in a friendly, open way with them. Your friendly behavior will almost certainly bring out friendly behavior in others, re-creating your past experiences and confirming your expectation that people treat you well.

This system works great if you have a past you want to re-create. However, if you would like to break free from the past and create a different future, this system can keep you trapped unknowingly. If you have had a lot of experiences in your past that you didn't like, chances are you are expecting the future to bring similar experiences, even if you don't want them. And you are acting in ways consistent with what you expect, thereby re-creating experiences similar to those past experiences you so disliked. The good news is that, once you are aware of it, you can stop this process and do something different. Your past does not have to define who you are or where you are going.

While we use our history to predict the future, it is not the only means by which we can create the future. We can become aware of this process as it is happening in the present moment. Once we are aware of it, we can intercept it and consciously choose to think new thoughts that have the potential to grow into new anticipatory beliefs. These new expectations will lead us to taking different actions that will create a different future. We can also use newly learned information about who we are today to help identify what we are capable of going forward.

Most people create their future by re-creating the past.

The other good news is that learning to create a future experience is a skill anyone can learn.[1] Research has shown that people who successfully do things to create their future, such as setting goals, planning, and solving problems, consistently experience greater well-being,[2] while people with fewer of these skills tend to experience more negative emotions, which can lead to serious conditions such as depression.[3] If you keep reading, this book will teach you the skills you need to break out of old patterns and habits so that, with a little effort, you can stop re-creating your past and improve your ability to make different choices and create more of the experiences you desire.

Kelly was in her early forties and had been unhappy in her marriage for many years. She largely depended on her husband's approval in order to feel good, and even slight criticism from him could land her in bed for several days. Kelly knew she had "married her father," who had been distant and critical while she was growing up. Kelly always worked hard at being perfect to avoid criticism, but when her strategy of being perfect failed, or she didn't receive the positive reinforcement she craved, she would spiral into bouts of negative emotion and self-criticism. Kelly had been in other types of therapy for many years, and she was easily able to recognize that she had re-created the relationship dynamics she had with her father and that she was acting in ways that were continuing the pattern with her husband. Yet she had never been able to break the cycle and do something different.

When Kelly began FDT, instead of trying to help her understand her past, the focus was on helping her identify a new pattern of future behavior, which included putting approval of herself over everyone else's opinions and seeing her husband as an equal, not as someone she had to work so hard to please. The plan for her treatment then became focused on teaching her the skills to help her achieve what she wanted and overcome the obstacles that were getting in the way. Initially she struggled with breaking her old patterns; she had difficulty creating a visual image of what it would be like to respond differently and to see herself as someone with more self-confidence. With practice, however, she developed the awareness to recognize when the old patterns were kicking in so that she could implement her new skills. This eventually led to improved self-esteem and a more equal and fulfilling relationship with her husband.

CREATING A NEW FUTURE EXPERIENCE

Creating a new future experience is not difficult. There are four basic steps. First, you have to initiate a thought about something you want that doesn't yet exist. For example, *I want a new job*. Next, you need to imagine what that job would look like. *I would like to be a manager at a retail company, not in sales*. Then you must anticipate the tasks necessary to make it happen. *I need to create a résumé that shows why I would be qualified to do this job; then I need to search the internet for open positions; then I need to mail my résumé*, and so on. Finally, you will need to execute the tasks you have anticipated. While these four basic steps may sound relatively easy, many obstacles along the way can trip you up.

In many ways, creating your future is like trying to lose weight. Everyone knows how to lose weight — eat less and exercise more. But people struggle every day with this issue because of the many complex barriers that get in the way; that is why helping people to lose weight is a multibillion-dollar industry. Likewise, everyone knows, to some degree, how to create their future because they do it all day, every day. But very few people know how to direct this process in a way that regularly leads to successful outcomes or how to get around the many barriers in the way. In the upcoming chapters you will learn how to approach life from a place of awareness and successfully complete the steps to creating a desired future experience, as well as how to overcome the roadblocks you may encounter along the way.

WHAT ABOUT THE PRESENT MOMENT?

The power to alter the course of your life lies in the present moment of awareness. However, we cannot hold on to the present moment. The present moment is what just passed. The future is always what is arriving. The now and the arrival of the future are one and the same, and you have tremendous power to influence the future that will arrive to become the now you experience.

A good deal of emphasis has been placed on "being in the present moment" by psychologists, popular-culture authors, and spiritual leaders, so much so that thinking about the future has gotten a bad rap. While being aware of thoughts and feelings in the present is an important skill, keeping your thoughts focused on the present moment by itself will not help you create a better future. If you want something different, you will need to think forward and plan for something different to arrive. While thinking about the future can cause fear and anxiety if you focus on the things you don't want, focusing on the negative is not an inherent component of future thinking; rather, learning how to think about the future in a positive, constructive way is essential to creating a life you desire. Being aware of the present moment gives you the opportunity to make conscious choices, but it isn't sufficient in itself to help you improve your future and what arrives in your experience. There is much more you need to know if you want to create true change in your life, so keep reading!

The Feeling of Thriving

The desire to thrive is a fundamental instinct that is always present. No one ever reaches a state where the desire to thrive ends. Even those whose profoundly difficult life circumstances have caused them to become frustrated, or to believe that thriving is not possible, continue to desire improvement in their experience. Each time we realize a desire that we believe will help us thrive, we gain a new vantage point from which another new want is born. For example, when you first started high school, you wanted to graduate; as time went on and you anticipated that achievement, you formulated other wants, such as getting a job or going to college. If you chose college, when you first showed up you probably just wanted to enjoy the experience; then, as time went by and you began to anticipate your college degree, you probably started to think about what other opportunities were now open to you, and you formulated new wants about what you planned to achieve next. Thriving is not a destination that we reach permanently fulfilled, but rather an ongoing experience of personal growth and evolution.

Thriving is subjective and relative. What you perceive as thriving and moving forward in life is completely defined by your set of circumstances, and it may be very different from someone else's idea of thriving. Someone who is starving wants to obtain a source of food; someone with an adequate food supply turns his or her wants in the direction of other increased means of thriving, such as safe and comfortable shelter. Thriving can include almost any human activity, such as building

15

strong relationships with others or improving our psychological or spiritual insight. For someone like Bill Gates, who has all that money can buy, the desire to thrive can take the form of feeling gratification from humanitarian efforts.

While thriving is a subjective state, one premise of FDT is that what people seek in life is the process of growth, including psychological, mental, and physical expansion. When something is too easy and doesn't challenge us, the reward we get from achieving it is low. When we achieve something that we work toward, we appreciate and value it much more.[4] For example, if you set a goal to improve your health by walking half a block a day, you may be able to achieve it with relative ease; however, your sense of personal gratification and accomplishment, as well as your body's physical improvement, will probably be significantly lower than if you had set the goal to run a 10K, trained for weeks, and then crossed the finish line in under your targeted time. Now you are on your way to reaching for your next target, which might be to run a marathon. Constantly reaching for increased states of thriving causes us to continue to grow and evolve as people.

When humans perceive that their survival or ability to thrive is being threatened in some way, they experience psychological distress and negative emotions. Your emotions act as an internal guidance system to let you know whether you are moving in the direction of thriving or away from it, as when the GPS tracking system in your car tells you that you are getting closer to or farther away from your intended destination. When we are in a state of thriving, we have a natural sense of psychological well-being. Here are a few examples:

Example 1. Social relationships are vital to the survival and thriving of human beings. When we have positive, strong relationships with the people in our lives, such as our parents, partners, children, or coworkers, we generally feel good about those relationships. When we are in conflict with others and our relationships with them are threatened in some way, we generally feel upset.
Example 2. Money buys us many things that promote survival and thriving. When people feel they don't have enough money, they generally start to feel anxious and distressed. How much is enough is a matter of individual perception, but when we believe there is *not enough*, we may feel great distress.
Example 3. Safety is essential to human survival and thriving. If we don't feel safe because we believe bad things will happen and we don't feel able to stop them, we are likely to experience distress and other negative emotions.

If you are experiencing psychological distress, that is an indicator that you are not thriving in some areas of your life. More important, you are most likely feeling uncertain or unhopeful about your ability to improve the situation in the future. As you continue reading this book, you will learn to identify thoughts and beliefs that you may be holding about your future that are keeping you from thriving, and, most important, you will learn how you can more effectively use your thoughts about the future to promote a sense of greater well-being.

How Can You Thrive More and Feel Better?

Feeling better doesn't just happen because you want it to. It will require that you do some work that may at times seem quite difficult. There are, however, certain things that you can do as you read this book to set the stage for your success. Read the following concepts carefully and try to absorb their meaning before moving on, because they are preconditions for successfully making a lasting change in your life.

Be Willing to Change

Without a willingness to change, there can be no better future. Change is difficult; the thought alone can inspire fear and anxiety. Many experiences in the past may be causing you to doubt that your life can ever be different or that change is even possible. These past experiences may have caused you to close yourself off from the things you really want. You may fear failure. You may believe that it is other people who should change. However, you are the only one with the ability to change your life and create a different future.

Willingness to change is not the same as wanting to feel better. Everyone wants to feel better, but many people are not willing to do what it takes to make that happen. Willingness to change means you are open to doing something different and learning a new way of being in the world. If you are open and willing, then change and new opportunities are possible.

Past experiences do not define who you are, unless you allow them to. You are free to change at any time. Many concepts and ideas in this book may challenge your way of thinking or your way of doing things, but if you approach them with an attitude of willingness, you will open yourself to the possibility of changing your life. The only thing you should be unwilling to do is to make your choices from a place of fear. When you are willing, you are facing a situation from a position of courage and strength. Be willing to let go of the fear and say yes to new possibilities. Before reading any further, close your eyes, take a deep breath, and ask yourself:

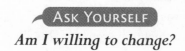
ASK YOURSELF

Am I willing to change?

ACCEPT RESPONSIBILITY

Everything you do matters! Every action you take, every thought you think contributes to shaping your future. Each of your thoughts and actions builds on others, generating thoughts and actions of a similar nature that eventually lead you to creating a new experience. If you begin to accept and recognize the significance of everything you do and of the choices you make, and if you treat each thought and action with the respect it is due, your life will begin to transform more rapidly than you could ever imagine.

The key to recognizing the fact that everything you do matters is taking full responsibility for all your thoughts and behaviors. There may be people in your life who have hurt you. Those people do not choose your thoughts or behaviors now. The past can only continue to hurt you if you allow it to. There is nothing more tragic than allowing people who have hurt you in the past to continue controlling your future because you refuse to give up believing that the unhappiness in your life is their fault. You are the only one with the power to change your life, but it is a responsibility that you must accept by recognizing that everything you do matters.

OWN YOUR CHOICES

The choices we make create our life. You cannot move forward without making some type of choice every moment along the way. If you choose to read the rest of this page, that is a choice. If you choose to stay in bed and pull the covers up over your head that is a choice. If you choose to go to the gym or to stay home and watch TV those are both choices. Everything we do and experience is dependent on the choices we make all day, every day. Even those with limited life choices, such as someone in a jail cell, can choose how to deal with that experience. Some prisoners become bitter and angry, while others choose to be productive and do things like obtain a law degree. The power to choose your thoughts and behaviors is the one right and freedom you are guaranteed.

Choices come from within. We can choose consciously, or we can choose on autopilot, in default mode. When choosing on autopilot, we do whatever comes most naturally to us because it is what we are used to doing. These types of choices are often so automatic that we barely have to think to make them. Your morning routine or your drive to work are things your probably do so automatically you can do them while you are still half asleep. There is very little conscious choosing happening; you are just doing what you always do.

Conscious choices, however, are what we make to change our life. Choosing consciously requires present-moment awareness. This doesn't mean that just because you are aware of your choices, making better choices is easy. It can still be very tough to make choices that go against familiar patterns. With awareness, a window of opportunity opens to do something different. You must, however, go through that open window. Many people sit on one side of the window staring through it, waiting for it to magically open or for someone to pick them up and carry them through. If change is what you desire, you are the one who must open the window and step through, using the power of your choices. No one else is responsible, and no one else can do it for you. When you own your choices, you own your power.

The choices we make move us either away from thriving or toward it. Learn to ask yourself regularly:

ASK YOURSELF
Where are my choices taking me?

PARTICIPATE IN THE PROCESS

One of the tricky things about creating your future is that you often won't be able to see how everything will unfold. You may have a general sense of where you want to be. You may even have some very specific goals; however, there are going to be many steps along the way that you won't be able to see until you start taking actions toward your goal. For example, if you know you want to go to college, you may not know which one is right for you until you start doing research to narrow down your choices. You may not know how you will pay for school until you explore the financial-aid options. You won't know which classes you will need to take until you meet with a counselor who can explain them to you. You won't know what you need to do to pass a class until you get there and wait for the professor to tell you.

While going to college is a very structured activity with concrete steps to take along the way, the path you need to take to achieve many of the things you want will often not be as clear. However, if you participate in the process and keep heading in the right direction, solutions you never thought of will start to unfold. As we will discuss many times in this book, your brain has a solution-generating ability that helps you solve problems, but you must activate this part of the brain by focusing on what you want.

Taking action is a key component of participating in the process. Even if you have no idea what to do to achieve what you want, simply following very small threads can open up new possibilities that you didn't even know existed. For example, if you want a new job but don't know what kind of job, you can start with what you know to do — go to a career counselor, read a book about your interests, take a career test, search an employment website until something of interest jumps out at you, talk to everyone you know about your desire to find a new career and ask them about all the different jobs they've had. All these activities can lead to new information, new ideas, and new directions. Keep following each new thread and see where it goes. As long as you participate, things will eventually start to happen and the information you need to make choices will start to appear.

STAY THE COURSE

There is always a span of time and distance between where you start and where you want to go. If you commit to your well-being and stay the course, you will get there. Many people turn around before they even arrive, then decide they want to try again, then turn back again, creating an endless cycle of trying and giving up. If you set out intending to drive from Los Angeles to San Francisco but turned around when you got to Bakersfield because you didn't like it there, then you would never make it to San Francisco.

The journey to well-being takes time, but once you arrive, you will find it has all been extremely worthwhile, and the field of psychology has well-tested maps to guide you. Along the way, however, you may find yourself in some places where you won't want to be. Because the journey to well-being is an internal journey, the places you don't want to be may include thoughts, beliefs, and emotions that you don't like. You may have to face old fears, deal with anger, or let go of beliefs that your lack of success is someone else's fault. If you stay the course, you can get past these places to find the well-being you are seeking; if you don't, you will end up back where you started. If you want to achieve greater well-being, you will need to commit to staying the course, and if you are thinking about turning around, just ask yourself:

ASK YOURSELF
Am I in Bakersfield?

Likely there will be many times when you feel like your efforts aren't getting you anywhere. Try to remember that just because you haven't yet arrived doesn't mean you are not making progress. Because we are in our bodies 24/7, we have difficulty noticing change as it is occurring, but change happens constantly. It is like your hair growing. From one moment to the next you don't notice the growth, but every three months you need a haircut! If you feel as if you've been putting forth your best effort but you are still not making progress, try asking someone you trust and know well if he or she has noticed any changes. It is often much easier for someone else to notice how you've changed, especially if they don't see you every day.

Be Aware of the Barriers to Progress

Stay aware of potential barriers to your progress. If you are prepared for them, you will be far more likely to deal with them successfully than if they show up unexpectedly. Let's look at some of these barriers in greater detail.

Mistaking Discomfort for Distress. Often, when you do something new, you experience what psychologists refer to as *cognitive dissonance*. In simple terms, since it isn't what you are used to, it *feels* wrong. But just because something feels wrong doesn't mean it is wrong. For example, if you are used to writing with your right hand, writing with your left hand will be really difficult at first, and it will feel wrong. You may have a very strong urge to switch the pencil back to your right hand. However, there is nothing wrong with using your left hand; it is just different and difficult because you aren't used to it. If you practiced for a while, you would get used to it, your writing would become more readable, and it wouldn't feel so strange.

So what would motivate you to keep practicing with your left hand? Not much, if there were nothing wrong with your right hand. However, if your right hand were broken or you had lost the use of it, then you would have strong motivation to tolerate the discomfort of using your left hand long enough to improve. The same is true of your thought process and your coping mechanisms. If things are working for you, then you won't have a lot of motivation to change them. Only when they are no longer working, and you experience psychological distress or an impaired ability to live the way you want to, will you have reason enough to try doing something different — which is probably why you are reading this book.

When you are used to doing something, it feels safe and comfortable, sometimes even when what you are doing isn't working for you. This feeling is called *being in the comfort zone*. For example, if you prefer to stay home instead of going to parties, being at home is your comfort zone. If, however, you decide that you would like to make more friends, you will have to acknowledge that staying home isn't helping you to achieve what you want. If you want to make a change, you will have to step outside your comfort zone and attend a few parties.

When you first step outside your comfort zone, you will likely experience fear, which is very normal. You cannot live without fear, nor should you want to. Fear alerts us to possible danger and tells us to prepare for it. You should also not just *feel the fear and do it anyway* unless you have assessed where the fear is coming from and decided that what you want to do is really in your best interest. What you need to do is learn how to *distinguish discomfort from distress*. Any time you step outside your comfort zone and do something new, you will experience some type of discomfort — that is the very definition of being outside the comfort zone. The good news, however, is that if it is just normal discomfort, and you can tolerate staying outside your comfort zone, you will eventually become comfortable in the new space, and your comfort zone will have expanded. In essence, your comfort zone will follow you, and each time you step outside it and tolerate the initial discomfort of the new space, you give your comfort zone an opportunity to grow.

A healthy level of discomfort is a form of anticipatory anxiety, which may even improve your ability to perform many activities. Discomfort should feel tolerable. When you are feeling discomfort, your chosen activity should still feel exciting and pleasurable to you. Anxiety becomes a problem, however, and creates *distress* when it starts to feel overwhelming and impairs your ability to function. For example, if you've always wanted to sing on stage but your anxiety overwhelms you so much that you completely freeze up, that anxiety is preventing you from achieving your goal. Distress tends to feel consuming and overwhelming; you may even experience physical symptoms such as a racing heart or a stomachache; you may feel panicked or as if you might die if you take the action. When you are in a state of distress, this is the wrong time to act. Your expectations of a positive outcome are likely not yet strong enough to carry you through successfully, and any unsuccessful experience will just reinforce any fears you have about doing something new. As you will learn in chapter 10, emotional alignment with a goal is one of the keys to success.

Distressful anxiety occurs when your thoughts about what you don't want in a situation outnumber your thoughts about what you do want. Distress is the result of focusing mostly on what could go wrong instead of what could go right. While the concept of how you allocate your thoughts will be covered in much more detail in the next chapter, for now you just need to know that doing something different can make almost everyone feel a sense of normal discomfort, but that discomfort doesn't mean you shouldn't do it if you believe it will bring you closer to what you want. If the anxiety starts to feel distressful, try to refocus your thoughts on all the positive reasons why you want to do what you are feeling anxious about. If that doesn't work, you may have stepped too far out of the comfort zone all at once, and you will need to pull back a little until the distress goes down to a tolerable level of discomfort. Just remember this rule of thumb — discomfort feels more good than bad — you may feel uncomfortable, but you are still really looking forward to where you are going. Distress, on the other hand, feels more bad than good — the negative feelings are overwhelming you and you can't even focus on your desired goal.

Casey was feeling ambitious about improving her life. She had been stuck in an emotionally abusive relationship for several years, and her boyfriend's constant criticism had eroded her confidence and deterred her from pursuing her dream of becoming a physician's assistant. Within six weeks of starting the FDT course, she had broken up with her boyfriend, moved into her own apartment, and signed up for a full load of medical science classes at a local college. She felt that since she was almost thirty she had no time to lose. Casey was excited about her newfound sense of empowerment and made lots of big leaps all at once, and while she was excited about her changes, she also started to feel overwhelmed and nervous that she was going to fail at school. She started having trouble sleeping at night, and she had recurring nightmares about being lost in a maze as she searched for her classes, unable to find them until the day of the final exam.

Casey was able to recognize that while she liked the activities she was pursuing toward the goal of thriving, the feeling of being overwhelmed and the nightmares she was having were more than just normal discomfort; they were obvious signs of distress, and she made the wise decision to take a step backward. She realized that there was no need to do it all at once and that smaller steps would still get her where she wanted to go, building her confidence in the process. Rather than taking a full course load, Casey decided that she would take one science class and one class that was just for fun, and she opted for an art appreciation course. With less pressure and a schedule that felt more doable, she was able to regain her excitement about the future, as well as her peace of mind.

I JUST DON'T FEEL LIKE IT. When you haven't felt yourself thriving for a long time, you may have developed a pattern of negative thoughts and emotions so entrenched that it can affect your health and lead to physical symptoms such as low energy, fatigue, and lack of interest in the things you used to enjoy.

When you are feeling really bad, it can be difficult to motivate yourself to do something, even when you know it is good for you. Feelings and behaviors, however, are two different things. While people's behavior generally follows from their feelings, it doesn't have to. You can choose a behavior that is different from how you feel. When you do so, often you can create a new feeling that is consistent with the behavior. If you behave as if you are feeling good, the feeling will follow, and soon you *will* be feeling good. For example, if your boss yells at you and you go home, eat a half gallon of ice cream, and go to bed, chances are you will feel even worse. If instead you go home, call a friend, and meet up at the gym for a yoga class, it is very likely that your mood will improve.

Often when you are down, it feels as if you just *can't* make yourself do the things you know you should do. It just feels impossible. The more you tell yourself you can't do it, the more this will feel true. However, *can't* is different from *won't*. If you felt like you couldn't get out of bed but someone offered you a million dollars to do so, you would quickly find the energy to leap right out. You can make yourself do lots of things, but you *won't* if you don't feel motivated. If you are depressed, you may feel less motivated to do the things you enjoy, but that doesn't mean you can't do them. Learning to focus on what you desire is a key task to be discussed in the chapters ahead. For now, when you feel unable to do things you know are good for you, ask yourself:

ASK YOURSELF
Could I do it if someone gave me a million dollars?

Keep in mind that you don't have to behave according to how you feel. When you don't *feel* like doing the practice assignments in this book, you will be able to do them anyway, knowing that practicing is what keeps you on the path toward greater well-being and a brighter future.

OLD BELIEFS. You are most likely reading this book because you are looking for a way to have greater control over your future. You have probably reached this point because what you've been doing up until now hasn't been working. As you work your way through the chapters in this book, you will be introduced to many new concepts and perspectives that may be very different from the way you have thought about things in the past. If you want to begin to feel better, you will need to remain open to new ways of thinking. Do not fight to hold on to your old beliefs just because you have always had them!

We human beings are capable of holding on to sincere beliefs that are not based in reality. For example, for thousands of years people believed the world was flat. People didn't plan exotic trips or travel very far from home because they were afraid they might fall off the edge of the planet. Today we know that the Earth is not flat, yet millions of people for thousands of years were limited by that false belief.

We know that people often hold on to beliefs about their futures based on beliefs formed from past experiences. But these beliefs may not be based entirely on facts that are true for you in the present, and they may be limiting your expectations and the choices you make about your future.

ASK YOURSELF
Am I limiting my future because of my mistaken beliefs?

Practice What You Learn

People don't make changes or move toward thriving unless they do something different from what they've been doing. You can see a psychotherapist for years or read an endless number of self-help books, but change will never happen until you put what you are learning into daily action. Learning the skills that promote positive future thinking and greater well-being is like anything else that requires practice, such as playing a musical instrument or shooting hoops. When you start out, you won't be very good. It may seem impossible that you could ever improve. However, if you practice consistently, you will get better and better at using your new skills until they start to seem like second nature. With consistent practice, you can take control of the direction you are heading, become the master of your own creative mind, and actively choose the future you create.

Embrace the Journey

While all this may sound like a lot of work, the good news is you don't have to arrive at a better place in order to feel better; you just have to be heading in the right direction. The *anticipation* of positive events by itself produces positive emotions. It is a mistake to think that you can't be happy until you have a better job, or a better relationship, or a new house. Psychological research shows that happiness can come as you make your journey toward the things you want.[5] When you believe the things you want are possible and your actions are moving you in the right direction, you feel hopeful. When you aspire toward growth, you feel motivated. The journey itself is what transforms you into the person you want to be. The struggles you encounter along the way provide the lessons that allow you to grow.

The key is to stay focused on where you are going and not on the fact that you haven't yet arrived. This book is intended to help you do just that, while also helping you acquire the skills to find the right path and make the journey go more smoothly. But alas, there are no shortcuts. There will always be travel distance between where you are and where you want to go. The journey, however, can be the very best part; it is what gives your accomplishments meaning and value. If there were no journey you wouldn't grow much as a person and you would soon be very bored. Embrace the journey and enjoy the ride. Whoever you are now is a very different person from who you are in the process of becoming.

The journey is what transforms you into the person you want to be.

PRACTICE ASSIGNMENTS

1. Complete the worksheet "Am I Willing?" on page 27. Write down three things you would like to change by the time you've finished this book. As discussed in the section "How Can You Thrive More and Feel Better?," wanting change and being willing to change are two different things. The people who achieve change are the ones who are willing. Go through each of the three items and read the five Ask Yourself questions.

   It is very likely that at this early stage in the process a lot of resistant thoughts come up as you go through these questions, such as, *I want to change but I feel scared* or *I want change but I don't believe it is possible.* Write down these thoughts. There are no right or wrong thoughts; this is about finding out where your resistance may be so that you can be aware of it. When you are aware of an obstacle and you prepare for it, you are far more likely to successfully get past it. How to get past the obstacle of resistant thinking will be addressed in later chapters.

Worksheet: Am I Willing?

What would I like to change in my life?	ASK YOURSELF	What thoughts come up when I think about these questions? Which of the five am I likely to have difficulty with?
Example: *I would like to have better relationships with the people in my life.*		*I am willing to do these things, but what if other people still don't like me? What if I change but no one else does?*
	1. **Am I willing to change?** I am willing to be open to learning new material and trying new behaviors.	1.
1.	2. **Am I willing to accept responsibility?** I am the only one who can choose my thoughts and behaviors in the present moment, which will lead to creating a better future.	
	3. **Am I willing to own my choices?** The choices I make are powerful and contribute significantly to the life I create.	2.
2.	4. **Am I willing to participate in the process?** I am willing to keep doing the exercises until I start to feel better.	
	5. **Am I willing to commit to staying the course?** I am willing to complete the FDT class and/or read the book through to the end, even if it seems hard sometimes.	3.
3.		

Worksheet 1.1

From *Think Forward to Thrive* © 2014 by Jennice Vilhauer, PhD

Tips for Thriving

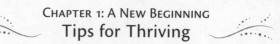

- Your thoughts are leading you either toward well-being or away from it, and your emotions are telling you in which direction you are headed. If you feel good, you know you are headed toward thriving and well-being.
- If you are experiencing negative emotions, it is because you are focused on some unwanted aspect of your life or some situation that is not leading you toward thriving.
- In the right frame of mind, you can start to feel better and set yourself up to be successful at changing your future.
  - Be willing to change: If you want something different, you will have to do something different.
  - Accept responsibility: What you do in the present moment creates the next present moment that arrives in your experience. Everything you do matters!
  - Participate in the process: If where you want to go seems unclear, the steps can unfold as long as you follow every thread and continue to search for the right path.
  - Stay the course: There is distance and travel time between where you are and where you want to go. If you turn around before you get there, you will never arrive.
  - Beware of the barriers to progress:
    - *Mistaking discomfort for distress.* It may feel strange to do something different, and it is normal to feel a tolerable level of discomfort. However, if stepping outside your comfort zone feels distressful and overwhelming, you should take a step back until it feels more tolerable. Discomfort feels mostly good; distress feels mostly bad.
    - *I just don't feel like it.* Thoughts and feelings are two different things. Your actions do not have to reflect your feelings. Even if you don't feel like doing the practice assignments, for example, you can still do them.
    - *Old beliefs.* Human beings have the ability to hold on to beliefs based on things that are not true. We form many of our beliefs early in life, and now that we are adults many of those beliefs are no longer useful to us. Because we create our future out of our belief system, it is worth considering whether you have any old beliefs that are limiting the choices you are making about your future.
- Practice what you learn!
- Embrace the journey. You don't have to arrive at a better destination in order to feel better; you just have to be heading in the right direction.

Chapter 2

THE VALUE OF YOUR THOUGHTS

That which dominates our imaginations and our thoughts
will determine our lives, and our character.
— RALPH WALDO EMERSON

Thought determines the direction we take in the journey of life and carries us into the future. It is the creative force of all human beings. There is nothing we can do without first thinking about it; thoughts power every choice we make and shape our very existence. Indeed, thought is our most valuable resource. However, because thoughts flow through our head all day long and may seem to be in endless supply, we are often not that aware of how we are "spending" them.

CONSCIOUS THOUGHT IS A LIMITED RESOURCE

We can think only a limited number of thoughts at any one time. Thought-flow studies have shown that, on average, we think about fifty thousand thoughts a day. Many of our thoughts are actually the same from day to day.[1] *Should I get out of bed now? What should I have for breakfast? It's time to walk the dog. What should I wear to work? Which route should I take to avoid traffic?*

Because thoughts are a limited resource, we need to choose how to spend them to ensure that we are getting what we want from them. How you spend your thoughts is very much like how you spend your money. You would never walk into a store, decide you didn't like something, and then say, *That's what I will spend my money on*, yet that's what many unhappy people do with their thinking. They spend a good deal of their thoughts on all the things they don't want and can't change, and they spend very few thoughts on what they do want and how they are going to achieve it.

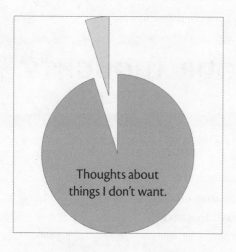

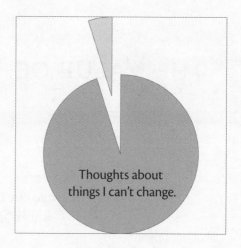

Imagine what your life would be like if you reversed the pattern and instead spent most of your thought process on how to improve your future and achieve the things you want. This is what successful, happy people do — people who get what they want out of life. They use their thought process wisely and spend it thinking about how to make what they want happen. Thoughts keep flowing through your mind all day long. Make the effort to have them flow in the direction that brings you the most benefit.

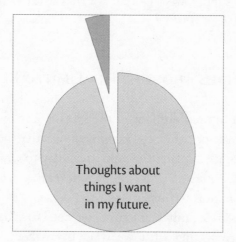

From *Think Forward to Thrive* © 2014 by Jennice Vilhauer, PhD

WE SPEND THOUGHT WITH OUR ATTENTION

When we purchase something with the limited resource of money, we generally make the transaction with cash, checks, or credit cards. The way we spend thought is with our attention. Attention is our level of conscious awareness that we can direct in order to notice or focus on something in our environment. We think about whatever we are focused on, and subsequently, attention is the gateway to what we experience.

Our attentional processing has a limited capacity, meaning we can only process a limited number of things at one time.[2] Because much, much more goes on in our environment than we could possibly pay attention to, the limited capacity of our attention creates the *illusion of awareness*.[3] In other words, while we think we are aware of all that is happening around us, in reality we are aware only of a small amount in our environment, and we are missing lots of other things without even realizing it. It is similar to the experience you have when you watch TV. There are way more channels than you could ever watch at one time; just because you aren't watching all of them doesn't mean they aren't there.

To maximize the limited amount of attention we have, our brains generate selective filters through a process called *priming*, which increases the brain's sensitivity to detecting certain things in our environment. Priming can occur intentionally or unintentionally, but in either case it tells the brain what to pay attention to.[4] You can think of the process of priming as a mechanism, similar to that of a TV, that allows you to selectively "tune in" to what you want to see. For example, you may have had the experience of purchasing a new car and then suddenly noticing that lots of people on the road seem to be driving your car as well. The reality is that all those people were driving those same cars all along. You just weren't noticing them until you primed yourself to notice them by purchasing the car yourself.

Here's another example. If you ask someone how many people he sees wearing red T-shirts every day, the average person will probably randomly guess a fairly low number, such as two or three. But if you ask someone to count, every day for a week, how many people he sees wearing red T-shirts, at the end of the week he will say he can't believe how many people wear red T-shirts. Without having been primed, he simply wasn't noticing, and the color of people's T-shirts was not entering his conscious level of experience.

Paying attention to one element in the environment not only activates brain processing of that element, but it also inhibits the processing of other elements by shutting down competing neural networks.[5] Someone looking for red T-shirts will see more people wearing red T-shirts and will pay less attention to what other people (those without red T-shirts) are wearing. Our level of attention actually determines the activity of the brain.[6] If we don't pay attention to something, even if it is present in our environment, it doesn't activate much brain functioning and we don't have much, if any, experience of it. Thus "we are not passive recipients...but active participants in our own process of perception."[7] How we direct our attention and spend our thought is critical to our experience of any given situation.

Karen was a retired schoolteacher who had encountered a number of difficult circumstances over the past few years. She and her husband had divorced, and her adult son had developed a serious drug addiction and lost his job as a result. She had spent the past three years getting into bitter arguments with her son whenever he asked her for money, while at the same time feeling overwhelmed with guilt as she watched him bounce in and out of rehab. Recently, her health had begun to deteriorate and she had developed symptoms of chronic fatigue and fibromyalgia.

When Karen first came for treatment, she was spending all day every day ruminating on her troubles, wondering where she had gone wrong. Her view of the world was quite bleak; if she wasn't discussing her problems, she would often describe negative things she had seen on the news or relate bad things happening to people she knew. Because Karen had a number of very real difficult situations in her life, it was hard for her to buy into the idea that she was participating in her situation by focusing her attention on the negative. So we started small. Karen's first assignment was to wake up every morning and count as many people smiling as she could in a day. She kept track in a little notebook. After three weeks, Karen came in to a session beaming. Not only had the number of people she noticed smiling increased steadily, but she had started to take notice of what all these people were smiling about. She told several very funny stories, then mentioned that she had shared them with others during the week and had a few good laughs with some of her friends. She said she had never noticed how many happy people were around her and how many things there were to smile about.

Nothing in Karen's life had changed — she still had the same problems as before — but because she was paying less attention to them and was instead intentionally focused on looking for something more pleasant, her emotional experience improved. This improvement led her to feel more optimistic that therapy could work for her, and she began to tackle the lessons with enthusiasm and dedication. Karen had to do a lot of hard work to find solutions to improve some of the situations in her life; however, her willingness led to action, which raised Karen's sense of well-being and the quality of her life.

THINKING ABOUT WHAT YOU DO WANT

What we want and what we don't want exist simultaneously in any situation; they coexist to provide contrast so that each can be known. To know that something is unwanted, we must know that something else is wanted instead. One serves as the reference point for the other. For example, we could not identify the wanted experience of happiness if we didn't know what it was like to experience the unwanted state of not being happy. If you know you don't want something, it is because you know that some other preferable state exists. If you decide you don't want a turkey sandwich, it might be because you want a cheese sandwich or because not having it just seems preferable at that moment, perhaps because you aren't hungry.

Given that the wanted and unwanted exist together, it makes sense that where you focus your attention and your thoughts determines your experience. Many people who experience negative emotions, such as anger and jealousy, by default are focusing their attention on what they don't want. For example, if you are invited to a party, you can focus on the aspects of the party you want, such as having a great time with friends, meeting new people, enjoying good food, and having an opportunity to relax, or you can focus on what you don't want, such as feeling uncomfortable with strangers, looking foolish if you decide to dance, not having the right thing to wear, or running into an ex-lover. Even in situations that might seem universally unwanted, such as getting a speeding ticket, you can focus on how lousy it is to get the ticket, or you can think about how lucky you are to have gotten a warning to slow down before something even more unwanted happened, such as an accident. You choose which experience to have.

Priming makes this process more automatic. The more often you tell yourself to look for the wanted aspect of a situation, the more your brain will start to selectively filter for what is wanted, increasing your ability to see the wanted things and inhibiting you from seeing the unwanted ones. When you notice you are having a negative emotion about something, realize you are focusing on the unwanted aspects of the situation and, if you want to feel better, simply start looking for any wanted aspect. Since they always exist together, which one you are seeing depends on where you are looking.

The goal is not to think positively all the time or to focus only on the things you want. That would be impossible. Thinking about unwanted things can help you give birth to new ideas and desires. For example, focusing on the unwanted event of global warming is inspiring scientists around the world to come up with new types of fuel sources that don't cause environmental pollution. Unwanted things are a part of life. When, however, we are able to redirect our thoughts toward wanted things and spend our thoughts on solutions, we continue to thrive. Your emotional experience of any situation depends on the proportion of your attention and thoughts you are focusing on both wanted and unwanted aspects. If you are focusing the *majority* of your thinking on the wanted aspect of a situation, you will feel more positive than negative about it. If you spend more of your thinking on unwanted aspects, you will feel mostly negative about a situation. Your goal is to tip the scale in your favor. If you want to feel good, search for as many wanted aspects in a situation as you can find.

If you are focusing the majority of your thinking on the wanted aspect of a situation, you will feel more positive than negative about it.

THE POLLYANNA GAME

Pollyanna is probably the most misunderstood fictional character of twentieth-century American literature. When most people think of a Pollyanna, they think of an overly optimistic goody-goody who doesn't see the harsh reality of the world. The term *Pollyanna* has taken on quite a negative connotation, and you frequently hear people using the term apologetically ("I hate to be a Pollyanna") or critically ("Stop being such a Pollyanna"). In fact, Pollyanna was not unrealistic or overly optimistic about anything. She was a little girl with a very poor but very wise father who recognized the duality of everything in life and taught her to play a game based on this idea. Pollyanna's game was known as the "glad game." One day Pollyanna's father, who was a church missionary supported by donations from the Ladies' Aid Society, received a long-awaited donation box for his family. Pollyanna, who had very few toys, had been wishing with all her might for a doll, but the only thing for her to play with was a broken pair of crutches. When Pollyanna started to cry, her father promised her that if she stopped crying he would teach her to play a game that would bring her more happiness than a doll ever could. He taught her that in every situation, no matter how bad it might seem, you could always find something to be glad about if you looked hard enough. Pollyanna and her father played the game every day, looking as hard as they could to find the thing they could be glad about in every situation. The more difficult the situation, the more fun and challenging it was for them.

After a while, the game became automatic to Pollyanna. She often didn't even realize she was playing it. She had just trained herself to see the wanted aspect in every situation. Pollyanna began to teach the game to everyone she met, and life-altering transformations started to occur for all who played. If you really want to start thriving, start playing the Pollyanna game. See if you can find an aspect to be glad about in every situation, no matter how bad things seem.

YOUR EMOTIONS ARE THE GUIDE

As you will learn about in more detail in the next chapter, thoughts come before feelings. When you are thinking on autopilot and not monitoring your thought process, you may be unaware of how you are spending your thoughts. However, your emotions will tell you every time. If you are feeling positive, you know that you are focusing on something that you like or want. If you are feeling negative in any way, you can recognize that you are spending your thoughts on something you don't want, and you can make an active choice about whether to keep focusing your attention there. Remember — where you spend your thoughts determines what you get in life, just like with shopping. Your emotions tell you whether you are making a good purchase or a bad one with your thinking. Don't you wish that kind of indicator were attached to your credit cards?

THOUGHTS GROW

Unlike with money, spending your thoughts *always* leads to a return on your investment. To make information retrieval easier, the brain organizes information both in hierarchies — such as pets, then dogs, then types of dogs — and in categories, such as fruits and vegetables.[8] Because of how information is stored in the brain, you can never just have one thought about something without activating a series of related thoughts. If you close your eyes and think of the color red for sixty seconds and then open your eyes and write down all the words you can think of, if you are like most people, you will probably come up with words like *apple*, *strawberry*, *Santa Claus*, *stop sign*, *wagon*. Why? Because you associate these items with the color red. In essence, thoughts generate similar thoughts, or to think of it even more simply, *thoughts grow*.

When you spend time thinking about negative things, your brain generates more and more negative thoughts. The good news is that the same thing happens with positive thoughts. The more positive things you think about, the more positive things your brain will start to retrieve that are associated with other positive things stored there. If you actively choose to focus on positive things, your thought process will eventually be dominated by good thoughts. This is also the case with time. The more you think about the past (which you can't change), the more thoughts of the past will keep coming up. If you redirect your thoughts to the future and your goals, more thoughts about the future and how to build that future will be generated.

If we focus on a thought about something we want, not only does it retrieve similar thoughts, but it begins to actually grow more thoughts about *how* to obtain it. One of the main purposes of the brain is to prepare for the arrival of the future, because this promotes our ability to survive. For this reason, the brain has a creative problem-solving function, called the "executive network," that generates solutions. This solution-generating part of the brain is turned on when there is an identified destination with a reasonable expectation of getting there. Later chapters will explain in more detail the very important role of expectation, but for now you are learning that whatever you focus on will grow a thought process around it. If you focus on an unwanted problem, your brain will grow more thoughts about the problem, and the problem will seem bigger. If you instead redirect your attention toward wanted solutions, your brain will generate thoughts to grow the solutions. Things you never thought of before will occur to you.

ASK YOURSELF

What new thoughts do my present thoughts generate?

REDIRECTING YOUR THOUGHTS

If you are experiencing emotional pain, it is because you are thinking about the unwanted aspects of a situation. Many people feel they have to resolve painful or difficult issues, and for that reason they spend too much time thinking about things that do not make them feel good. As just discussed, one of the primary premises of FDT is that thoughts grow. What you think about gets bigger. When you think about painful things, it brings more painful emotions. You can habituate yourself to a painful thought by thinking or talking about it so much that it starts to lose some of its sting, in the same way that your nose starts to lose its sensitivity to a smell. But while your nose gets used to a smell after about three minutes, the process is much slower with your thinking. All of us, however, once we develop the awareness, have the power to redirect our thinking away from a painful thought almost as soon as it occurs. Some people feel that when they redirect their thoughts, they are simply distracting themselves or avoiding the issue. In FDT, however, redirecting your thinking constructively is not the same as avoidance; in fact, it is one of the most positive coping strategies that you can develop! While there are times when looking back at an unpleasant event to figure out how it could have gone better or how you could do it differently in the future is very useful, allowing yourself to ruminate on painful events can cause significant distress.

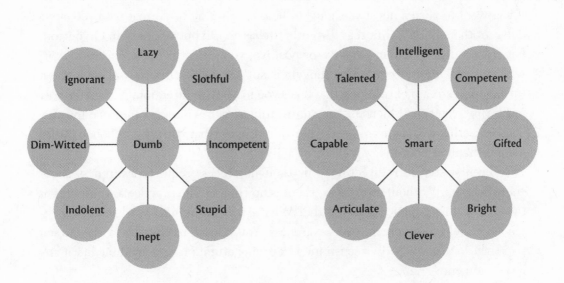

When we activate a thought, similar thoughts grow.

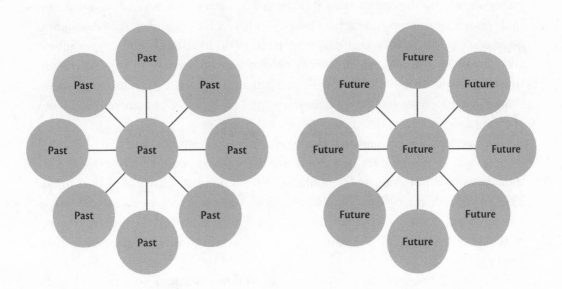

From *Think Forward to Thrive* © 2014 by Jennice Vilhauer, PhD

One of the reasons why redirecting your thoughts is so important is that the neurons in your brain work on an activation/inhibition model.[9] When you activate one neuron, that inhibits the activation of a competing neuron. When you activate a positive thought, that inhibits the activation of a negative thought, and vice versa. If you want to turn a negative thought off, the only way to do that is to activate a different thought. It is almost as if your brain has no Off button, only an On button. For any thought to occur, negative or positive, you must turn it on, or activate it, with your attention. Redirecting thought is not just distracting yourself; it is about turning on a stream of thinking that takes you in a better direction. No matter how much time you spend focusing on painful things, you will never improve the way you feel until you learn to redirect your thinking to what you want. Though it may seem difficult at first, everyone has the ability to do it.

The first step in redirecting your thought process requires awareness about your thoughts. Without awareness, there is no choice. The practice assignments at the end of this chapter, including the "What Am I Thinking?" worksheet, are intended to help you increase your awareness. You'll learn to check in with yourself regularly so that you grow accustomed to paying attention to your thoughts at any given moment.

Redirecting does not mean stopping your thought process. If you tell yourself to stop thinking about something, you are likely to think about it even more. I want you to think about a pink elephant. Now stop thinking about the pink elephant. Hmm, what are you thinking about now? You're probably still thinking about the pink elephant. Instead of trying to stop your negative thinking, the goal is to find something else to think about that is more in line with your desires. If you wake up in the morning thinking about how much you hate your job and all the reasons you don't want to go to work that day, your feelings of dread will grow bigger unless you actively choose to focus on something else. As you become aware that you are thinking about something unwanted, you can actively decide to refocus on something more pleasant, which will help you start to feel better and prevent you from growing more negative feelings.

Redirecting does not mean thinking the opposite, either. If you don't like your job, the goal is not to start thinking about how much you do like your job; this thought wouldn't be true, and it would feel almost impossible to hold in your mind. The goal of redirecting is to simply move your thought process to a subject that is more pleasant. Doing so accomplishes two things. First, it stops the negative stream of thoughts, and second, it changes the direction of the thought pattern you are growing.

You can do many things to redirect your thinking. Bringing your thoughts back to the present moment, which you will learn more about in chapter 6, is one technique. You can use the worksheet "My List of Positive Ways to Redirect My Thinking" on the next page to help you keep a list of the things you know generate

WORKSHEET: MY LIST OF POSITIVE WAYS TO REDIRECT MY THINKING

Subject	How does it make me feel?
Example: *My cat*	*I love my cat because he is warm and fluffy and because every time he sees me he brushes against my legs and starts purring. He makes me feel great.*
Example: *Love*	*Love is my favorite subject because, when I think about feeling loved and giving love, it makes me feel warm and fuzzy inside. I like thinking about the people I love. Love is a beautiful emotion.*
1.	
2.	
3.	
4.	
5.	
6.	
7.	
8.	
9.	
10.	

Worksheet 2.1　　　　　From *Think Forward to Thrive* © 2014 by Jennice Vilhauer, PhD

positive feelings, such as your dog or eating ice cream or the memory of your daughter's first laugh or a party you are looking forward to. You can also keep a list of your favorite words — such as *love*, *friendship*, *peace*, and *beauty* — and use those to refocus your thinking. One simple and highly effective technique is to start with the first letter of the alphabet and think of something you like that starts with that letter, like apple pie. Then go to the letter B and find a word for something you like that starts with that letter, like beauty. Keep going until you get to Z. By then you will have completely forgotten any negative thoughts you were having.

Another great technique for redirecting your thinking is to practice gratitude. When you focus on what you are thankful for, you are thinking about things you want that already exist, so this is a great place to spend your thoughts if you want to quickly improve your mood. As you will read about in the next section, your eventual goal, as you work through the chapters, will be to learn to actively redirect your thinking toward the things that you want. What is important to know right now is that even if you have no idea what you want, you can redirect your thoughts *away* from things that generate negative emotions so that you are not growing more of them.

REDIRECTING YOUR THOUGHTS
TO YOUR IMPROVED FUTURE

From the FDT perspective, the single most important thing you must do to improve any unwanted situation is to identify a desired solution, a place you would rather move to. This place becomes your identified future destination, no matter how near or far that future is.

Once you have an identified desired destination, a cognitive dilemma is created: *How do I get from point A, where I am, to point B, which is where I want to go?* When you ask yourself this question, in order to solve this dilemma the problem-solving part of the brain, the executive network, gets activated. As discussed earlier in this chapter, attention is a key method for activating the brain. The more attention you allocate toward getting to point B, where you want to go, the more active the problem-solving part of the brain becomes as it works to come up with a way to get you there. This is because if B is a desirable state, focusing on B increases the motivation to get there. For example, if you have the thought *My life is stressful (point A) and I'd like to go on vacation (point B)* and then go back to focusing on all the stressful things in your life, the likelihood of your going on a vacation is low. If, however, you stopped focusing on the stressful events in your life and instead redirected your thoughts toward how to take a vacation, your brain's problem-solving mechanism would go to work and start to generate solutions to help you get there. You would start to think of places you would like to visit; then you might start to look up some of those places online, and as you did this, you would start to visualize what it would be like to actually be in those places.

Perhaps you would imagine yourself lying on a warm, sandy beach in Tahiti sipping a refreshing drink. The more you thought about this, the more motivated you would feel to get there. If you believe you can get to Tahiti and the drive is high enough, you are likely to take some action toward making it happen. Whenever you find yourself faced with a situation you don't like or want, rather than focus on it, stop and ask yourself:

ASK YOURSELF

Where do I want to be instead?

A——> ——> ——> ——B

How can I get there?

All solutions come from asking some version of these questions. Once you have identified a target, you have something to work toward, and as you begin to spend your precious resources of thought and attention on your intended destination, your brain will go to work to help you get there. As you will learn more about in chapter 4, because we human beings spend resources only on what we believe to be possible, you need to choose a point B that you think you can realistically get to, not somewhere that's far out of your reach.

While having fantasies about things you know to be impossible can make you feel good in the short term, the goal is to create a destination you can work toward so that you can turn it into a reality you live. Learning to close the gap between where you are and where you want to be will require the use of many skills, which you will acquire as you keep reading. However, simply giving more of your attention to point B and spending thought there can lead to rapid improvements in how you feel about any situation. As long as you have something to look forward to that feels like an improved condition, there is hope — and hope is what we thrive on.

Hope is what we thrive on.

EXAMPLE 1: STACY

Point A ———> ———> ———> (Where I am)	———> ———> ———> **Point B** (Where I want to be)
Stacy was recently diagnosed with breast cancer and felt very scared.	Stacy wanted to get through the treatment and get her health back to better than it ever was before.
Thoughts generated by focusing attention on point A	Thoughts generated by focusing attention on point B and asking: *How can I get there?*
1. *Why is this happening to me?* 2. *Bad things always happen to me.* 3. *I should have taken better care of my health.* 4. *What if the treatment is painful?* 5. *I can't cope with this. I already have too much stress in my life.* 6. *Am I being punished?* 7. *What if I die?*	1. *I need to talk to other women who have survived breast cancer.* 2. *Maybe I can find a support group.* 3. *I will talk with my doctor about all the possible treatment options.* 4. *I will make a list so I don't forget any important questions.* 5. *I also want to explore nutritional options.* 6. *I will talk with my friends and family and ask them for extra support.*

EXAMPLE 2: ERIC

Point A ———> ———> ———> (Where I am)	———> ———> ———> **Point B** (Where I want to be)
Eric was a small-business owner with a problem employee whom he couldn't trust.	Eric wanted to let go of the problem employee and find a competent replacement.
Thoughts generated by focusing attention on point A	Thoughts generated by focusing attention on point B and asking: *How can I get there?*
1. *This is so lousy. I hate dealing with things like this.* 2. *He is probably robbing me blind.* 3. *I am such an idiot for hiring this person.* 4. *I should have known better. I screw up at everything.* 5. *Working for myself is so stressful.*	1. *I have a long list of justifiable reasons why I should fire him.* 2. *Things will run so much more smoothly when he is gone.* 3. *I will post an ad online to find someone better.* 4. *I will make sure to get a background check on the next person I hire.* 5. *It will feel great to be rid of this guy.*

From *Think Forward to Thrive* © 2014 by Jennice Vilhauer, PhD

EXAMPLE 3: SALLY

Point A ———> ———> ———> (Where I am)	———> ———> ———> Point B (Where I want to be)
Sally was having an argument with her husband, about his excessive drinking, that was turning into a screaming match.	Sally wanted to communicate her concerns to her husband in a calm, loving way.
Thoughts generated by focusing attention on point A	Thoughts generated by focusing attention on point B and asking: *How can I get there?*
1. *He doesn't care about my feelings.* 2. *I hate it when he doesn't listen to me.* 3. *He is an insensitive jerk.* 4. *I am so incredibly angry.* 5. *This feels awful to be fighting.* 6. *I can't stand living like this.* 7. *Why did I marry him?*	1. *I am going to stop discussing this and do something else until I calm down.* 2. *My therapist said I should focus on my feelings and not blame him. So I will try that.* 3. *I need to listen and understand his perspective and not only focus on my concerns.* 4. *I know he doesn't want to fight either.* 5. *I love my husband.*

From *Think Forward to Thrive* © 2014 by Jennice Vilhauer, PhD

WORKSHEET: MOVE YOUR THOUGHTS FROM POINT A TO POINT B

First, write down any problem or unwanted situation in your life. Really focus on the problem, what you don't like about it, and why it makes you feel so lousy. Write down the thoughts that come to mind. Then ask yourself: *Where would I like to be with the situation instead?* Come up with something that feels like a realistic improvement or a resolution to you. It doesn't have to be anything big or grand. Something like *I want to feel calmer in this situation* could be a great place to start with point B. Then ask yourself: *How can I get there?* Focus on that for a few minutes and write down what thoughts come to mind. If there are resistant thoughts like *I can't do this, it will never happen*, don't worry—we will discuss how to get past that type of thinking in chapter 5 on overcoming resistance.

Point A ——> ——> ——> (Where I am)	——> ——> ——> Point B (Where I want to be)
Thoughts generated by focusing attention on point A	Thoughts generated by focusing attention on point B and asking: *How can I get there?*
1.	1.
2.	2.
3.	3.
4.	4.
5.	5.
6.	6.

Worksheet 2.2   From *Think Forward to Thrive* © 2014 by Jennice Vilhauer, PhD

PRACTICE ASSIGNMENTS

1. Increase your awareness of your thoughts. This week, place Post-its in your bedroom, bathroom, and kitchen, on your television, and in your car with the words: *What am I thinking now?* Every time you see one of these Post-its, pause and take a breath, then check in with yourself and observe your thoughts. When you do this, ask yourself:

ASK YOURSELF

Is this what I want to be spending my thought process on?

2. Complete the worksheet "My List of Positive Ways to Redirect My Thinking" on page 39. Simply follow the example and list a few things that make you feel good; then write a sentence or two about why each one improves your mood. Make sure to place the list somewhere accessible so that you can take a look at it whenever you start generating negative thinking. Your refrigerator, your purse, and your wallet are all great places.

3. Try the exercise on moving from point A to point B with your thinking on page 44.

4. To further practice what you've learned and to increase your awareness of your thoughts, complete the "What Am I Thinking?" worksheet at the end of the chapter, on page 46.

Worksheet: What Am I Thinking?

Each morning when you get up, and each night right before you go to bed, spend a few minutes thinking about the dominant thoughts running through your mind. What are they? What time frame do they have to do with — past, present, or future? How are they making you feel? Is this something you want or don't want to spend thought on?

Weekday	Thought	Past/Present/ Future	Feeling	Want/ Don't Want
Sunday				
Morning	I don't want to get out of bed and go to a job I hate.	Future	Depressed	Don't want
Evening				
Monday				
Morning				
Evening				
Tuesday				
Morning				
Evening				
Wednesday				
Morning				
Evening				
Thursday				
Morning				
Evening				
Friday				
Morning				
Evening				
Saturday				
Morning				
Evening				

From *Think Forward to Thrive* © 2014 by Jennice Vilhauer, PhD

- Thought is a valuable, limited resource. Spend it on what you want, not on what you don't want.

- We spend thought with our attention. What you focus on determines your experience.

- Check in with yourself regularly to see where you are spending your thoughts.

- When you are feeling down, play the Pollyanna game. Look for some wanted aspect of the situation, something you can be glad about, no matter how difficult circumstances may seem.

- You can grow your thoughts just by paying attention to them, so grow thoughts about what you want out of your life.

- Learn to redirect your thinking away from what you don't want and toward any topic that makes you feel better as a way to immediately improve your mood.

- Carry your list of positive items with you everywhere, and pull it out whenever you need it.

- When you are in an unwanted situation, spend your thoughts on creating a point B place of improvement that you can work toward.

Chapter 3
COMPONENTS
OF THE HUMAN EXPERIENCE

The first step toward change is awareness.
—NATHANIEL BRANDEN

Though we have spent a good deal of time talking about our thought process, there is more to life than just what we think — there is also how we feel, what we do, and what we experience. All these aspects play a role in how we create our future. While your thoughts have a profound influence on all components of the human experience, understanding each of the components and their relationship to one another is an essential part of gaining greater control over your future.

INTERPRETING OUR ENVIRONMENT WITH ANTICIPATION

Research in the last decade has given psychologists a new understanding of how the brain works. We now know that the brain primarily operates on a predictive model.[1] In order to adapt to our ever-changing environment, we have to be able to predict effective responses. As a result, many of the brain's primary functions are wired to help us anticipate the future so we can be ready for what we expect to occur. While this may sound perfectly logical and perhaps even obvious, the fact that we live in constant anticipation of what *will* happen has profound implications for how we interact with our environment and create our lives. We often respond to what we think will happen and not to what in reality is happening. When we act in response to what we *expect*, we participate in shaping the events that occur.

A simple illustration of the brain's power of anticipation can be seen in optical illusions, which are created by the anticipatory nature of the visual system. There is a delay of one-tenth of a second between what we see and our brain's ability to process that information. To make up for that delay, the brain compensates by anticipating one-tenth of a second into the future what it believes it *should*, based on stored information, not what it is really seeing.[2] As a result, we experience optical illusions.

Visual illusions are an example of the brain using anticipation
to process environmental information.

*When we act in response to what we expect, we participate
in shaping the real events that do occur.*

The lines extending from the black dot in the center of the image cause our brain to anticipate forward motion. The apparent bending of the two vertical lines in the center is caused by the brain's expectation that you are getting closer to the center, and therefore the lines appear farther apart. Even though the image does not move, your brain is anticipating forward movement; the illusion occurs because you are seeing what your brain is preparing to see, based on what it expects to see, not what is really there.

What we anticipate creates a filter through which we view the world and shapes what we experience. Because a small time lapse occurs between the moment something happens and the moment our mind perceives what is happening, our brain has learned to anticipate what we believe *should* happen in most situations. When we expect things to happen in a certain way, we prepare ourselves for those events. We may start to feel certain emotions or take certain actions before the expected event happens. Because we often start to respond before an event even occurs, we play a big role in influencing what really happens. For example, if you were hurt in a previous relationship, you may expect that you will get hurt again, and it would be natural to act in a guarded way with a new partner. However, if you are guarded and can't open up, you may push your new partner away. What you anticipate about an event is the pivotal point in the process that sets the future you create into motion. While we can anticipate an experience quicker than the blink of an eye, it is a multistep cognitive process.

The way we think about our world follows an organized pattern. First, we perceive an event and interpret it through an existing belief system; next, we anticipate what the event means for our future, even if that future is just a moment or two away. As part of the process of anticipation, we evaluate whether what we expect will move us toward thriving or away from it (i.e., is it something we want or don't want?), and subsequently, it triggers an emotional response. We then generally choose to take action according to how we feel. While there are a lot of steps here, this process can happen so rapidly you often aren't even aware of it.

For example, if you see a dog running toward you, you will interpret that event through your existing belief system about dogs. If you have previously had a positive experience with dogs, you will have one belief, but if you have had a lot of negative experiences with dogs, you will have a very different belief. As you see the dog coming toward you, you will anticipate what it is going to mean for you when the dog arrives (a future experience) based on your past experiences. If you believe that dogs are friendly, you will expect this to be a positive experience, but if you believe that dogs are dangerous, you will expect this to be a negative experience.

Your ability to form preferences will help you determine whether the experience you expect is something you want or don't want. If you are expecting a negative experience with this dog, that is something you won't want, and it will be marked by some negative emotion, such as fear, that tells you this is not a situation that promotes your thriving. You will then need to decide what to do. Your brain will need to choose from an array of possible choices what action will move you back toward thriving. *Should I run away? Fight the dog? Pray for help?* Your brain has to calculate, through the process of anticipation, which response or action is in your best interest. When this process is happening in real time, especially in a situation in which danger is involved and your survival is threatened, the action part of the response may come before you are even aware of the emotion.

What you anticipate about an event is the pivotal point in the process that sets the future you create into motion.

FDT ANTICIPATORY COGNITIVE MODEL OF HUMAN EXPERIENCE

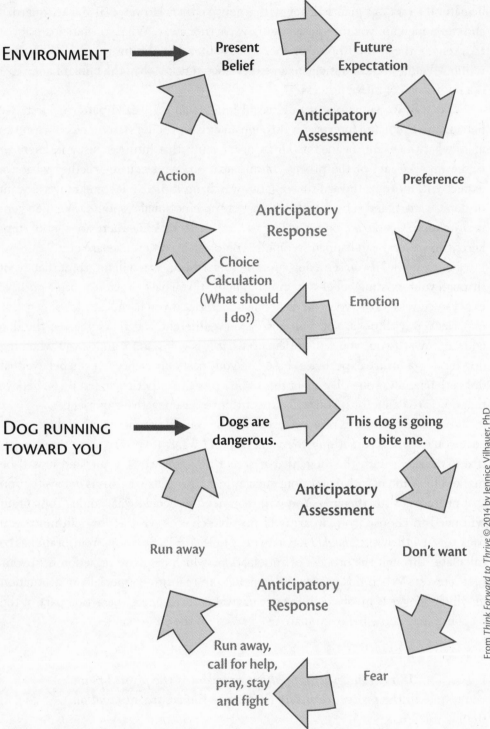

From *Think Forward to Thrive* © 2014 by Jennice Vilhauer, PhD

WHAT CREATES OUR EXPERIENCE?

The more you understand the relationship between these components of the human experience and how they work together to produce your future experiences, the more you will be able to actively make choices about your thinking, choices that will help you gain greater control over your emotional well-being.

ENVIRONMENT

Environment is anything happening around us that we are consciously aware of. It can refer to an event such as a wedding, news such as finding out that we have an illness, external experiences such as another person's behavior, and so on. The list is endless. We can also become aware of things in our internal environment, such as a racing heart or even our own thought process. When we are talking about our own experience, we tend to think of things that happen in our environment as situations or events.

BELIEFS

Beliefs are stored points of view that we think are true, based on experience. While beliefs are constructed from our thoughts they are not quite the same thing. We all have thoughts that we do not believe. For example, you can have thoughts about a monster hiding in your closet but not really *believe* that a monster is there. Beliefs generally come from patterns of thought that have been repeated over and over until we accept them as *true*. That does not mean that they are true. Human beings are capable of holding on to beliefs that are not based in reality or truth (remember the world-is-flat example from chapter 1); however, something in our experience must cause us to accept a thought as true in order for it to be a belief. We filter the information in our environment through our belief system and make interpretations about what events mean for us based on what we believe.

FUTURE EXPECTATIONS

Expectations are a particular type of belief about the future. They represent what you think will happen in the future or what you think the world *should* look like in the future. That doesn't mean it will be that way, but it is what you expect will occur. Because we are constantly moving forward into the future, we interpret present-moment events based on what we expect they will mean for the future, even if the future is only the very next moment. Because it hasn't happened yet, this is the place in your experience where you have the most power to change your life. When you are operating on autopilot or in default mode, your expectations are automatically generated from your stored beliefs. If you then act in anticipation of what you expect, you usually end up re-creating a situation similar to a past one, without even realizing that you are doing it. If you do not wish to re-create the past, once you are aware of the process you can change what you expect so that it is more in line with what you want.

Changing what you expect can dramatically shift how you feel and what you do, which will result in different experiences. The goal is to develop awareness in the present moment about what you are expecting so that you can make better choices and anticipate experiences that are consistent with what you want. The present moment is the window of opportunity allowing you to step out of the past, choose to do something different, and begin to create a better future.

Past	Present Moment	Future
Old Experiences *What you've learned*	Beliefs *What you think is true about your world*	Anticipations *What you are expecting and preparing for*
Can't Change	Window of Opportunity *You can become aware of your thinking and choose something different.*	**Hasn't Happened Yet** *This is what you influence the most.*

*The present moment is the window of opportunity allowing you
to step out of the past, choose to do something different,
and begin to create a better future.*

PREFERENCES

We assign preferences to what we expect.[3] We assess — *do I want this or not? How much do I want it or not want it? A little or a lot?* Our ability to discern our preferences, or to identify what we want and what we don't want, is essential to knowing what moves us toward or away from thriving. We prefer things that lead us toward a perceived state of increased thriving based on where we are in any given moment. We evaluate all expectations of the future through our preference filter, which allows us to decide whether events are moving us closer to or farther away from what we want. Preferences are what allow us to assign value to something in our environment. We can have a great preference for something — *I really want the double-fudge chocolate cake over the eggplant* — or a weaker preference, such as *I prefer Thai food to Chinese, but I'll happily eat either one.* Preferences can be very obvious or very subtle. For example, you may prefer a high-paying job to a low-paying one because a high-paying job will increase your ability to buy things that help you thrive. You may also prefer one song on the radio to another because it elicits an emotion that brings you closer to the emotional state you desire at the moment.

Your preferences can change over time. Thriving is both a subjective and a dynamic state. As you will read about in chapter 7, there is a hierarchy to our preferences that influences our choices and is based on what we value. For example, you can prefer ice cream to spinach but also prefer being healthy to being overweight, so you may choose the spinach because you value your health most highly in this scenario. The actions you take, however, are also determined by where you are focusing your attention as you make the choice. In order to take an action that is consistent with your values, you have to focus on the benefits of what you value; otherwise, you may choose the equivalent of the ice cream.

FEELINGS

Feelings, referred to interchangeably as emotions, are a response to what we have been thinking. While we may not always be aware of our thoughts about something, if we stop and pay attention, we can generally tell what kind of emotional state we are in — at the very least, we can tell whether we feel mostly good or mostly bad. Feelings are very much like the indicator lights on the dashboard of your car — if you are out of gas, the low-fuel light will turn on. If you are focusing on something unwanted, a negative feeling will show up. Your emotional state indicates what you are giving attention to, even if you are not aware of it. When you are experiencing a negative emotion, ask yourself:

> **ASK YOURSELF**
>
> *What am I thinking about that is making me feel this way?*

Our feelings serve as a guidance system, signaling whether movement toward or away from something is in the interest of our survival and/or thriving. When what you are anticipating feels like something you don't want, your internal guidance system is telling you that you should probably avoid that thing. The stronger our feeling about an event is, the more we perceive it to be moving us in one direction or another. For example, love is a strong emotion that moves us in the direction of thriving; fear is a strong emotion that signals potential danger. Events that cause strong emotions can really hold our attention, and subsequently redirecting attention away from topics that generate a lot negative emotion can require a good deal of effort.

Emotions exist on a continuum. People often make the mistake of thinking they can feel only negative or positive emotion. The truth is there are many feelings in between, including the feeling of being neutral or calm.

Negative			Neutral			Positive
Depressed	Angry	Anxious	Calm	Excited	Happy	Joyful

Whether or not your emotions are pointing you in the direction of thriving has to do with where you start on the subject. For example, if you are depressed because your boss yells at you, and then you start to feel angry because you realize you shouldn't have to tolerate this behavior, then the anger will feel like movement toward thriving because it is a step up from depression. However, if you are feeling happy with your relationship with your boss, and then your boss starts to yell at you and you get angry, that is going to feel like movement away from thriving because you have moved down the emotional continuum from where you started. Paying attention to the changes in your emotions can tell you which direction you are going in based on where you started.

CHOICE CALCULATION

Before we act we have to choose from an array of possible actions what we are going to do. If you experience fear in response to something in your environment, you can make many choices. You can avoid the feared object, you can engage it, you can use denial and pretend it doesn't exist, you can ask for help with dealing with it. But how do you decide? The full answer is somewhat complex. We know from the field of neuroeconomics, the study of human decision making, that one of the primary things we do is calculate a cost-benefit analysis for the possible alternatives and then choose the option with the greatest perceived benefit at the most minimal cost. However, since we are making rapid decisions most of the time, our brain can't possibly calculate all the possible choices, so it takes a shortcut by calculating from what is most active in the brain.

For example, a very religious woman who went to church every day was mugged by a man one day as she was walking home from church. As he yanked the purse off her arm and started to run away, she could have made several choices; she could have simply let him take the purse and then called the police, she could have screamed for help, she could have held on to the purse and fought back. What she chose to do, however, was to tell the man that he was a blessed son of God and that she promised to pray for him every day. The mugger turned around and handed her back her purse, then ran away.

The action she took was not the choice that most people would have made. So how did she come to take this action over the other options that most other people would have picked? For this woman, because she was quite religious, God and prayer were very active in her thought process. They were something that she gave attention to many times throughout her day.

As we know, what you give your attention to activates the brain. Because thoughts about God and prayer were so active in the woman's mind, they were very present for her in calculation about what to do in a situation where she felt threatened. She believed God was her protector and that he would always help her. In her mind there was a very high value in turning to God for help which, again, in her mental calculations, superseded the benefit of the other choices she could have made.

When we are choosing in autopilot mode, we base our calculations largely on what is most recently active in our mind. If you don't like the choices you make, it is easy to look back later and wonder why you didn't make a different choice, but that is often because the benefits of the other choices weren't present in your mind at the time you made the choice. It doesn't mean that you didn't know about the other options; it just means they weren't active enough for rapid retrieval. Think about the process of deciding where to go out to eat. You may have come across a new restaurant you see that looks good, and think *That's a place I'd like to try*, but a week later, when a friend puts you on the spot and says, *Hey, where do you want to go for dinner?*, chances are what comes to mind are the same places you always go. That's because those places are the most active in your mental space.

Again, attention plays a critical role in what is available to us when we make decisions. If you want to lose weight but spend time watching cooking shows on TV and thinking about all the delicious food you would miss out on, you are not focusing on the benefits of losing weight, so when you try choosing between chips or carrots, chips will likely seem more appealing. If you are working on a particular goal, you can actively prime your brain with the information that will help you make the best choices toward reaching that goal.

BEHAVIORS

Behaviors are physical responses we make based on our thoughts and feelings; they include activities, interactions, and postures. Behavior generally follows from how we feel — *I feel sad, so I stay home and don't go to the movies with my friends*. What we often don't realize is that our behavior has a big effect on how we feel. When you feel sad and choose to stay home from the movie, you may end up feeling alone and isolated, which increases the feeling of being sad. People who behave as though they are depressed feel depressed. If you feel sad but choose to go to the movie anyway and spend time with your friends, you will probably feel better. Behaviors are separate from our feelings, and we can choose behaviors that are different from how we feel.

HOW DO THE COMPONENTS WORK TOGETHER?

The components of environment, beliefs, expectations, preferences, feelings, choice, and behavior make up all your experiences. They interact continually, leading us to anticipate an expected outcome, which often reinforces old patterns. Here is an example:

- **Environment:** Jane gets invited to a party at the last minute.
- **Belief:** Jane believes that last-minute invitations are not sincere and that the person who invited her doesn't really want her there.
- **Future expectation:** Because of her belief, Jane expects that, if she goes, she will have a bad time.
- **Preference:** Jane decides this is not something she wants.
- **Feeling:** Jane starts to feel sad about the situation.
- **Choice:** Jane has several options. She imagines that if she goes it will be unpleasant, and that staying home would allow her to avoid an unpleasant situation. She stops there and doesn't consider other options.
- **Behavior:** Jane decides to stay home.

As you have learned, and as you can see from this example, the beliefs we hold in the present influence what we anticipate about the future. Jane believed the invitation wasn't sincere, and as a result, she expected to have a bad time. The process of anticipation led her to generate an emotional response about the event that was consistent with her expectation, long before the event ever occurred. If she went to the party anticipating that she would not have a good time, Jane would likely show up in a bad mood and choose a consistent behavior, such as sitting in the corner and not talking to anyone, and then go home thinking, *I knew I would have a bad time.* She would conclude that her original belief had been correct, and now it would be stronger than ever, even though her behavior was what created the negative experience.

We can interrupt this process of reinforcement by becoming aware of our beliefs and the expectations we have of future experiences. Once we have awareness, we can generate new ways to look at the future that bring us closer to what we want. For example, if Jane had recognized that her negative anticipation was causing her to feel bad, she could have consciously chosen to anticipate something more positive, such as having a good time at the party, whether or not she was invited at the last minute, and then focused on generating ideas for how she could enjoy herself there.

Because the components of our experience are interconnected, changing any one of them will influence the others. If Jane had a different belief — such as, *Last-minute invitations are a great opportunity to do something fun and unexpected* — all the subsequent components in the interaction would have changed. Jane likely would have anticipated a positive experience, which was something she wanted, and her behavior also would have changed, because she would have gone to the party expecting to have a good time and would have been friendly with other party-goers. Jane had no reason to change her existing belief, which she felt she had good evidence for, based on her past experiences. On the other hand, Jane could still maintain her belief about last-minute invitations but recognize that expecting to have a bad time wasn't going to get her what she wanted, and instead consciously change her expectation to something more positive: *Last-minute invitations might be insincere, but if I go to the party, I will still have the opportunity to meet lots of new people and I can have a good time anyway.* Changing what she was anticipating, even without changing her present belief, most likely would have changed Jane's behavior and the resulting emotion in turn, and she would have opened herself up to the possibility of creating a better experience.

While we are not always in control of what happens in our environment or of what other people think and do, we do have the ability to observe and modify our behavior, shift our attention, and change our thinking, particularly our thinking about the future — which can profoundly change what we experience. If you catch yourself anticipating something unwanted, stop and ask yourself:

ASK YOURSELF

Is there something I want more that I could choose to expect instead?

Taking charge of your future starts with being aware of what you are thinking in response to events in your life. Once you are aware of your thought process, you will be able to decide whether you want to maintain negative expectations that are not helping you get what you want, or to act in alignment with a more preferable outcome.

PRACTICE ASSIGNMENTS

1. Complete the "Components of My Experience" worksheet on page 61 to begin identifying the components of your experiences that you have the power to change.

WORKSHEET: THE COMPONENTS OF MY EXPERIENCE

Learn to identify the components of your experience by breaking down emotional events in your life so that you can begin to recognize the various components and identify the ones you can choose to change. While you can choose any events from the past, present, or future, it is generally easier to work with more recent or near events, such as in the past or upcoming week, because you will be better able to identify all the components.

Example.
Environment/Situation: *A dog is running toward me.*
Belief: *Dogs are dangerous.*
Future Expectation: *The dog may bite me.*
Preference: *Don't want/Not thriving*
Feeling: *Scared*
Choices: *I could run or stay, but running seems safer.*
Behavior: *Run away*

1.
Environment/Situation:
Belief:
Future Expectation:
Preference:
Feeling:
Choices:
Behavior:

2.
Environment/Situation:
Belief:
Future Expectation:
Preference:
Feeling:
Choices:
Behavior:

3.
Environment/Situation:
Belief:
Future Expectation:
Preference:
Feeling:
Choices:
Behavior:

Worksheet 3.1 From *Think Forward to Thrive* © 2014 by Jennice Vilhauer, PhD

Tips for Thriving

- The seven components — environment, beliefs, future expectations, preferences, feelings, choices, and behavior — make up your experiences. They interact continually, often leading to patterns that reinforce themselves or create what we commonly refer to as self-fulfilling prophecies. The more you pay attention to this process as it is happening, the more choices you will have.

- Stop and notice as you experience your environment. Remember that everything you think and do is leading to the creation of some new future experience.

- Notice whether what you anticipate is creating something you wish to occur.

- Observe whether your actions are reinforcing old beliefs. Could you take a different action that would lead to something you would rather experience?

- As you become more familiar with observing the various components of the human experience, in any situation make sure to notice whether what you are expecting is what you want. If it is not, you can consciously decide to expect a more desirable outcome and then purposefully choose your behavior and act accordingly.

Chapter 4

Creating New Expectations

The best way to predict the future is to create it.
— Abraham Lincoln

Despite the fact that most of our beliefs are based on past experiences, it is not what we believe about the past that matters; rather, it is what we believe our future will be like because of those past events that determines the course of our life. For example, if in your past you have failed at things you've tried to achieve, those failures don't affect your future *unless* you anticipate future failure because of them and then limit your choices and actions because you expect to fail again. As we know, when we anticipate something, we prepare for what we expect to occur. What we anticipate is the foundation on which we build our life.

It is not what we believe about the past that matters; rather,
it is what we believe our future will be like because of those past events
that determines the course of our life.

We Prepare for What We Expect

If you decide to lean against a wall, you are probably expecting that the wall is solid and will support you. Your expectation is based on a stored belief that walls should be solid because walls in your past experience have always been solid. If you leaned into a wall and suddenly discovered it was soft like Jell-O, you would be very surprised and would probably fall into it feeling really silly. The interesting question here is, *Why* would you fall? You would fall because you were expecting something solid, so that was what you prepared for. You adjusted your muscles, and the weight and position of your body, in a way that prepared for the present-moment experience of leaning against a solid wall. This is an example of how we live every moment of the day, in everything we do. We prepare for what we expect. If we expect good things, we prepare for good things; if we expect bad things, we prepare for bad things.

Because we anticipate things based on past experiences, we generally expect things in the future to happen the way they did in the past. We behave according to what we expect, and our *behavior* often brings about the expected result, which reinforces our original belief. This is an example of a *self-fulfilling prophecy*. For example, if you didn't get a good evaluation in your first annual review at work, you may expect your boss to view you as incompetent, and as a result you may feel nervous and anxious whenever your boss is around. If you feel nervous and anxious, you may make mistakes or say silly things you don't mean. If your boss seems to notice these behaviors, or if she comments on them, you will likely interpret that as a confirmation that your boss does not think you are competent. You are likely to say, *See, I told you so*, but in reality it was what *you* expected and how you then behaved that brought about the comments from your boss.

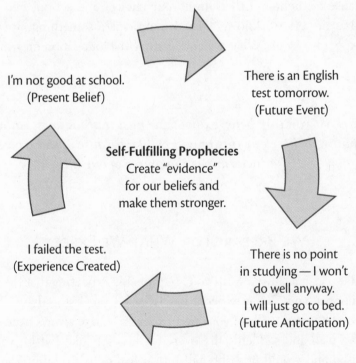

I'm not good at school.
(Present Belief)

There is an English
test tomorrow.
(Future Event)

Self-Fulfilling Prophecies
Create "evidence"
for our beliefs and
make them stronger.

I failed the test.
(Experience Created)

There is no point
in studying — I won't
do well anyway.
I will just go to bed.
(Future Anticipation)

From *Think Forward to Thrive* © 2014 by Jennice Vilhauer, PhD

BELIEFS LIMIT FUTURE EXPERIENCES

Action, like thought, is a limited resource because we can only take so many actions in any given time period. To maximize our use of this limited resource in a way that promotes our survival, our brain has adapted so that it only wants to take action on things we believe are true. Taking action on things we don't believe are true would be a huge waste of resources. For example, if it is 95 degrees outside and your partner tells you to take a coat before you go out because you might get cold, you are not likely to waste the time looking for your coat because you don't really believe you will get cold. However, if it is the middle of December and you look out the window and see snow on the ground, you will probably look for your coat because you believe that being cold is likely.

Because of our need to conserve resources, we take action based on what we expect, not what we want. If you have been bad at sports your whole life, you likely believe that you are not athletic, and the chances that you will invest any action in trying to become an Olympic athlete are very low, even if that is something you want. As another example, most people would like to win the lottery, yet few people buy lottery tickets on a regular basis. The reason for this is that most people don't expect to win, so they can't rationalize spending the resources required to obtain a ticket, even though they would really like to win.

We take action based on what we expect,
not what we want.

To get a better sense of how the past affects future experiences, read the past experiences and resulting beliefs in the table on the next page, then rank the likelihood of occurrence as low or high for each of the associated future experiences.

Past Experience	Present Belief	Future Experience	Likelihood
I got an F on my math test.	I am not good at math.	I will apply to college to become an engineer.	Low
I went to a party, and no one spoke to me.	I'm not good in social situations, and people don't like me.	I will ask out the next cute guy or girl I see.	
I was a cheerleader in high school.	People like me, and I am beautiful.	I will move to Hollywood to try to become an actress.	
I was fired from my last job.	I'm not such a great worker, and I'm lucky to have any job.	I will apply for a promotion to be a manager.	
My mother died of breast cancer at a very early age.	Breast cancer is hereditary, and I am likely to die of it early too, so there is no point in having kids.	I will try to have the large family I always wanted growing up.	
No one in my family ever went to college.	I don't belong in the college crowd.	I will work at a job that doesn't require a college degree.	

From *Think Forward to Thrive* © 2014 by Jennice Vilhauer, PhD

ASK YOURSELF

Are my beliefs limiting my future experiences?

Erin was a nurse who had been unemployed for four years. She was fired from her last job for making a serious mistake in medications with one of the patients she was caring for. Erin believed the mistake was a result of her incompetence, and she had spent the past four years ruminating about the event, feeling guilty and worthless, which brought on a major depressive episode. Erin had been too afraid to look for a new job because she expected to make a similar mistake in the future; also, she didn't know how she would explain her four-year absence from the workforce, which she expected would be perceived negatively by a new employer. Erin was miserable with her life; she felt she did not have a sense of purpose, and she missed the nursing work she had done for twenty years. Erin's beliefs and expectations were limiting her actions and preventing her from moving forward.

OUR EMOTIONS ARE THE PRESENT-MOMENT GUIDE TO THE FUTURE

When you act unconsciously, you generally end up re-creating whatever you have experienced in the past. You can, however, become aware of your future expectations by learning to pay attention to your emotions. As we've seen, your emotions act as your internal guidance system and are a direct reflection of what you are thinking about. To review, if, when you think of a future event, you have a positive emotion, you know you are expecting something positive to happen; on the other hand, if, when you think of a future event, you experience emotions like fear, anxiety, a sense of being overwhelmed, or a general sense of hopelessness, you can be certain you are expecting something you don't want.

If you use your emotional guidance system to identify what you are anticipating, you can consciously decide to act in accordance with what you *want*, not with what you have learned to expect. For example, if you believe you are not good at relationships because your past relationships have not worked out, you may anticipate that future relationships will not work out either. As a result, you may feel reluctant to engage in another relationship, and when you start to get close to someone, you may experience a lot of fear or anxiety. If you want to keep re-creating past experiences, all you have to do is keep acting in accordance with the negative emotions, and another relationship will probably end poorly. On the other hand, if you would like to create a different future experience with a more positive outcome, you can pay attention to the emotions of fear and anxiety, note them as signals of a negative expectation you are holding, and choose to expect something different about the situation, something that you would actually like to see occur. A thought more consistent with what you want in the future might be *I work hard to make my relationships turn out well.* Once you have chosen a new expectation that is more consistent with what you want, you can align your actions with the new expectation and do something different, such as reading a book on good relationship skills or taking a workshop on building better relationships. Your different actions will start to result in different outcomes. When you notice you are expecting something you don't want to occur, stop and ask yourself:

ASK YOURSELF
What do I want instead?

Although you project your expectations of the future from what you believe to be true in the present, and while it can be helpful to identify and/or change your present beliefs, doing so is not essential to changing your life or how you feel. Remember, the present is always leaving, and the future is always arriving. What is essential is that you change what you are expecting about the future experiences you are creating. As you change your expectations and take actions that are consistent with these expectations, you will start to create new experiences that are inconsistent with your old way of thinking. In the light of new evidence, the old beliefs will gradually start to fade away. To gain a better understanding of how we create self-fulfilling prophecies from our beliefs about the future, read the exchange between a client and therapist below.

Client: I lost my job today. (Environment)
Therapist: How do you feel about that?
Client: I feel sad and depressed. (Feelings)
Therapist: What are you thinking about losing your job that makes you feel depressed?
Client: That I am such a loser. (Present belief)
Therapist: You think you are a loser — hmm. What does that mean for your future?
Client: I'll never get another job; my wife will leave me; my friends will think poorly of me. (Future expectation)
Therapist: It sounds as if you think the future is going to be terrible. Is that what you want?
Client: No! Of course not. (Preference)
Therapist: What are you planning to do when you go home tonight?
Client: Probably go to bed because I feel miserable. (Choice)
Therapist: How will your wife feel about that?
Client: She'll probably be mad because she wants me to go to dinner with the neighbors tonight.

Therapist: So you believe the future is bleak because your wife will leave you and your friends will think poorly of you, and you are planning to go home and act in a way that will likely increase the chances that your wife and friends will be upset. Do you see that you are planning to act in a way that is consistent with what you believe about your future, which increases the likelihood that your belief about the future will come true?

Client: I never thought about that.

Therapist: Because you act on your beliefs, your beliefs create your future.

Client: But I can't help it if my beliefs are true.

Therapist: If those negative things you are anticipating didn't happen, would you still be a loser?

Client: No, I guess not.

Therapist: So your belief is only true if events in the future confirm your belief?

Client: I never thought of it that way. By going to bed and upsetting my wife and friends, my actions are what make my belief seem true.

Therapist: Yes, we call that a self-fulfilling prophecy. How many times do you think you've taken actions that end up creating experiences that confirm your negative beliefs?

Client: Probably lots.

Therapist: Do you see why you are so convinced your beliefs are true?

Client: I'm starting to. So what should I do to break the cycle?

Therapist: Why don't you start by telling me how you would like to see your future instead?

Client: You mean just make it up?

Therapist: You made up the first scenarios easily enough. Those things haven't happened yet; they just came to you easily because they are consistent with what you have thought about yourself in the past. But in order to take different actions, you have to start believing that something else is possible in the future.

Client: Okay. I would like to believe my wife won't leave me.

Therapist: That would be a nice thing to believe, but do you think your beliefs control her actions?

Client: No...but you told me to make up a belief I would rather have.

Therapist: Yes, but keep in mind that the beliefs that lead to your actions are the ones that count. The underlying belief you held was that you are a loser because you lost your job and your future will be terrible because of it. What part of the belief about yourself or your future actions could you try to change?

Client: I can probably get another job.

Therapist: And how would someone who can get another job act in this situation?

Client: They would probably see this as an opportunity and go home and start looking for one, maybe even a better job.
Therapist: Is a better job what you want for your future?
Client: Yes.
Therapist: When you think about having a better job, how do you feel?
Client: Good. I like the idea of having a better job. My old job really wasn't that great.
Therapist: Excellent! Let's start brainstorming on what you need to do to make that better job happen.

How Do You Identify Your Expectations about the Future?

To review, when we experience something, we interpret the event through a stored belief system, formulate a future expectation about it, decide whether or not it is something we want, and then have an emotional response to it. We only experience emotion in the present moment, so while at any given time we may be thinking of events in the past, the present, or the future, how we feel about them can only be experienced in the now. Because we can only move forward in time, we tend to be very concerned with how events will affect our future. Many of our feelings in the present are about how we expect events that have happened, are happening, or are going to happen will affect our life going forward.

Here are some examples of how events in the past, present, or future can cause you to experience negative emotions because of the negative experiences you anticipate those events will bring.

Past experience: My boss yelled at me two days ago.
Present belief: My boss doesn't like me very much.
Future expectation: I will never get a promotion, and I might get fired.
Preference: Don't want.
Feeling: Sad, upset.

Present experience: My car breaks down.
Present belief: When my car breaks down, I have to deal with a lot of unwanted difficulties.
Future expectation: I will have a hard time getting to work. I will have to pay a lot of money to fix it.
Preference: Don't want.
Feeling: Angry, upset.

Future experience: I have to discuss child-custody arrangements with my ex.
Present belief: He/she is always such a jerk.
Future expectation: This will be a very unpleasant conversation.
Preference: Don't want.
Feeling: Anxious, angry.

When identifying a future expectation, you often start with just a feeling. If you are feeling good, there is no need to change your thought process, so generally you will be looking for negative emotions — *I feel upset* or *I feel angry* or *I feel depressed.* Sometimes you will know clearly what event your emotion is connected to, but other times you will have to pause and ask yourself, *What thoughts are causing me to feel this way?* Doing so requires tuning in to the internal dialogue in your head, and this may take some effort. However, keep in mind that there is an event and a thought process to explain every emotion. The exercises from chapter 2 and the mindfulness work in chapter 6 will help you increase your awareness of what you are thinking about.

If you notice that the negative emotion you are experiencing is sparked by your thoughts about a future event, such as *I am likely to do poorly at the job interview next week*, this tends to be a bit easier to work with because there is some distance between where you are in the present and the future event. If you notice the negative emotion is sparked by an event that is occurring in the present, such as *I am angry at the very slow driver in front of me*, stop and ask yourself what you expect the present event to mean for your future. *Why does it matter?* For example, you may be expecting, *This slow driver is going to make me late for work* or *I'm going to miss an important appointment.* If there were no future consequences whatsoever, the slow driver probably wouldn't bother you so much. And even if you are reacting to a past event, you are thinking about what that past event will mean for your future. For example, if your boss yelled at you two days ago, you may still be upset and experiencing negative emotions over it today. Why? Likely because you are worried about some negative impact that event could have on your future at work — *I may not get that raise I was hoping for. What if I get fired?* Or perhaps you are very sad about someone in your life who has passed away. You may be thinking that your future life will be empty and lonely without that person.

Identifying what you believe an event means for your future is vital if you want to change your life and improve your emotional well-being. On page 72, write down any significant events you can think of. Identify whether the events are from the past, present, or future. Then identify how you believe the events will affect you in the future (remember, the future does not have to be far away). Label that expectation as something you want or don't want, and write down how that expectation makes you feel.

WORKSHEET: IDENTIFYING FUTURE EXPECTATIONS

Event/Situation	Past/Present/Future	Future Expectation What am I expecting will happen?	Want/Don't Want	Emotion
Example: My boss yelled at me.	Past	**Future:** I won't get a promotion, and I will always be stuck in this lousy job.	Don't want	Depressed
1.		**Future:**		
2.		**Future:**		
3.		**Future:**		
4.		**Future:**		
5.		**Future:**		

Worksheet 4.1

From *Think Forward to Thrive* © 2014 by Jennice Vilhauer, PhD

WHICH EXPECTATIONS ABOUT YOUR FUTURE SHOULD YOU HOLD ON TO?

The purpose of learning to be more aware of your expectations about the future is to gain the ability to create experiences that are enjoyable and that help you thrive.

Once you start to identify your expectations, it may sometimes seem very obvious which ones aren't helping you create a better future. Future expectations such as *I will never be good enough* or *No one will ever love me* should certainly be replaced. But other times it might not be so clear. When you are in doubt about whether a belief you hold about the future is one you should keep or replace, here is a question that can help you decide:

ASK YOURSELF

Will what I believe about the future help me get what I want?

If the answer to this question is no, you have a choice to make — either you will need to give up what you want, or you will need to give up your limiting belief about the future and replace it with a more effective one. You can do this by using the "how to create a new expectation" process detailed later in this chapter. Remember, we act on what we believe to be true. You can't achieve what you want if you don't believe it is possible.

WHAT IF YOUR NEGATIVE BELIEFS ABOUT THE FUTURE ARE TRUE?

Nothing about the future is guaranteed to be true, because it hasn't occurred yet. There is only what we think will occur, based on what we know about the present and past.

Truth is often a more subjective state than most people realize. We often think that if we can just find the evidence for something, it must be true. However, as we've discussed, much of the time we create supporting evidence for our beliefs through self-fulfilling prophecies. We also tend to filter the information in our environment so that we pay attention only to the information that confirms what we believe and disregard evidence to the contrary. As you create your future, always remember that what is true of the past does not have to be true of the future.

While you may have to contend with certain facts when you want to accomplish something, those facts may or may not limit you, depending on how you think about the situation. For example, someone who has had a leg amputated might think it impossible to participate in a marathon, and many people might agree. However, people in wheelchairs complete marathons all the time. When the desire is strong enough and the focus is on finding a way, the brain's creative problem-solving function goes to work on finding solutions. If you believe that you are limited by what is "true," then you are. If, instead, you would like to learn how to create new beliefs and expectations about your future, ones that will help you achieve more of what you desire, then keep reading!

HOW TO CREATE NEW EXPECTATIONS ABOUT THE FUTURE

Your future is like a canvas that you paint on, and your existing belief system is the paint palette. If the only colors on your palette are dismal shades of gray, it is very hard to paint a brighter picture. In essence, you need new paint, or new beliefs about your future, in order to create a more positive picture. When your expectations about the future don't paint a picture you are looking forward to, you will need to learn how to change your expectations.

There are three steps to creating a new expectation:

1. Initiate a new thought about the future.
2. Detail what that thought might look like until you begin to feel it is real or possible.
3. Take action consistent with the details of your thought.

INITIATE A NEW THOUGHT

A belief of any type starts with a single thought. The first step to creating a new expectation about the future is to come up with a new thought, one that is more consistent with what you want. Remember, thoughts and beliefs are not the same thing. We are all capable of having thoughts we don't believe. Because a thought is not a belief until it has been repeated many times and reinforced through action, you will probably not fully believe the new thought. It may even feel strange or awkward at first. Keep in mind that, when you start coming up with new ways of thinking about a situation, the thoughts and behaviors you try to alter must be your own. While you may not like someone else's behavior, you only have control over yourself and how you think and feel.

Once you have formed the thought you would like to turn into a new expectation about the future, write it down in a present-tense form, as though it is already true. For example, if you struggle with low self-esteem and your future expectation is that you will *never deserve a good life*, you might want to start with something like *I am a valued and worthy human being*. The reason the thought should be phrased in the present is that, as discussed, your mind is always projecting into the future based on the thoughts you believe to be true now. When you are criticizing yourself, you don't say, *I will become stupid, so I might not get the job*; you say, *I am stupid, so I might not get the job*. It is also far more powerful psychologically to say, *I am* than *I will*. There is more commitment to the statement, and as you say it, you conjure an image of that person already existing.

Another essential thing to keep in mind as you begin to create new thoughts is that not all thoughts are equal. Every subject can be viewed from two perspectives — that of *presence* or that of *absence*. You always want to initiate thoughts that imply the *presence* of what you want. When you make a statement like, *I want a boss who doesn't abuse me*, you are making a statement that implies the absence of abuse but not the presence of anything else. When you think of things from the absence-of perspective, you generally use words that include *no* or *not*, such as *won't, can't, will not, doesn't*. You may very well be trying to get rid of a thought you don't want; however, by replacing a thought like *I am afraid* with *I won't be afraid*, you don't imply the presence of anything other than being afraid. You want to make a statement that implies the presence of something else, such as *I am brave*.

Another example would be *I want a partner who doesn't lie*, as opposed to *I want a partner who tells the truth*. The first statement implies only the absence of lying, while the second statement implies the presence of truth. Because thoughts activate similar thoughts, you want to initiate thoughts that include the presence of what you want so that other thoughts associated with what you want become activated as well. As you will learn in chapter 9, your brain has only the ability to visualize the presence of things, and being able to see what you want in your mind's eye is a vital step toward achieving anything.

As you choose a new thought to turn into a future belief, the easiest way to succeed is to reach for a new thought that *feels* like an improvement over your old one but is not so far away that the leap seems too large to take. As you will see in the next chapter, when you try to make big changes in your belief system all at once, you end up creating a lot of internal resistance. For example, trying to go from *I am a loser* to *I am a winner* is too big a leap to take all at once and will most likely elicit thoughts such as, *Who am I kidding?* Try reaching for a new thought that feels like an improvement but not a huge leap, such as *Sometimes when I try, I do succeed*. Some phrases that may help you to choose improved thoughts without leaping too far include:

- I am capable of...
- I can learn to...
- I am working on...
- I can start...

- I can be aware...
- I am trying...
- I've done it before so I can do it again...

Finding a thought that doesn't require taking too big a leap is more difficult than it looks. Most people, when they first try this exercise, automatically go for the finish line, from *I am a loser* straight to *I am successful*. Naturally, you need to know where the finish line is. If you start off believing you are a loser, you may indeed want to move toward believing that you are a successful person. However, if you start with *I am successful*, you won't believe it at all. You want to start this process by reaching for thoughts that are within the realm of things you can believe about yourself. If you start with *I am a loser*, you want to reach for a thought like *I am someone who works on building better self-esteem*. You may need to try out a few different thoughts to find one that resonates on some level of believability. You can think of it like trying on a new T-shirt or dress — pick one out and ask yourself, *Does this one fit?*

You are a multidimensional being with a life of many facets, including work, love, play, and perhaps spirituality. Some areas may require that you work harder to change your thinking than others. While you may be ambitious about wanting to change your whole life at once, it would be wise, since you are just starting this process, to focus on the area that is of most concern to you. Once you feel comfortable with the steps of creating a new future expectation, you can work on the other areas and begin thriving in every aspect of your life.

You can use the "My New Thoughts about My Future" worksheet on the next page (p. 77) to practice creating new thoughts about the different areas of your life.

CREATE DETAIL

Now that you have a few new thoughts to work with, you will need to learn to *grow* the thoughts so that they become the basis of desired future experiences. Remember, the more you think about something, the more similar thoughts you will start to generate, and the more real and possible your new thought will begin to seem. Working with just one thought at a time, you will now begin the process of growing your thought into a new future belief by creating as many details about your thought as possible. The process of creating details leads you to spend your valuable cognitive resources on that thought and starts it on the way to becoming a new belief.

WORKSHEET: MY NEW THOUGHTS ABOUT MY FUTURE

Work	Love	Play	Spirituality
Example: *I have a job that I like.*	**Example:** *I build satisfying relationships.*	**Example:** *I find time to enjoy myself.*	**Example:** *I take the time to care for others.*
1.	1.	1.	1.
2.	2.	2.	2.
3.	3.	3.	3.
4.	4.	4.	4.
5.	5.	5.	5.

Worksheet 4.2

To begin, close your eyes and formulate a visual image of your new thought. Use as many details as possible to envision what it would look like if your thought were already a present reality. You can create an image of almost any future experience, as long as you've followed the guidelines in the section on initiating new thoughts. Even if your new thought is about a *feeling* you want to have, such as *I feel calm*, you can still create a visual image for yourself of what it would be like if you were feeling calm. Perhaps you would see yourself sitting quietly in a peaceful setting.

Then, building off your visual image, create a list of five details about your new thought every day for the next week. After seven days, you will have thirty-five descriptive points about your new thought. Once you have this list, your new thought should feel much more tangible to you, and you will be on your way to creating a new belief about your future. The main objective here is to begin to grow your thinking around your new thought, to make the possibility of it seem more real, and to provide you with areas in which you can begin to take action, which is the next necessary step in turning your thought into a new future expectation.

One way to grow detail around a new expectation is to ask yourself questions about what it would be like if it were already true. Again, you are going for detail, so no question is too insignificant. As an example, using the thought we initiated in the above section — *I am a valued and worthy human being* — begin to imagine what being a valued and worthy human being would look like by asking yourself:

1. What does a valued and worthy human being do?
2. What does a valued and worthy human being feel?
3. What does a valued and worthy human being wear?
4. What does a valued and worthy human being eat for breakfast?
5. What does a valued and worthy human being do for leisure?
6. What does a valued and worthy human being read?
7. How much time does a valued and worthy human being spend taking care of him- or herself?
8. How much time does a valued and worthy human being spend exercising?
9. What kind of internal dialogue does a valued and worthy human being have?
10. What kind of dreams does a valued and worthy human being have?
11. What kind of friends does a valued and worthy human being have?
12. What kind of friend is a valued and worthy human being?
13. How does a valued and worthy person communicate?
14. What kind of music does a valued and worthy human being listen to?
15. How does a valued and worthy person manage his or her money?

Once you've written out a list of questions and answered them, look for evidence that any of these details you have created already exist in your life. For example, look to see if you are already doing some of the things you have written down. Perhaps you already read books that are about developing your mind, or you already dress in a way that is consistent with how you think a valued and worthy person dresses. As you look for the evidence that the new belief you are trying to create already has a foothold in your life, you will find that you are on your way to transforming your new *thought* into something your truly *believe*.

TAKE ACTION

What you tell yourself programs your actions. Our minds make decisions about what actions we are going to take before we are even consciously aware of the action. Some studies have shown that our brains use whatever is stored there to make predictions and decisions several seconds before we are even aware of our decisions.[1] Whatever is stored in our brain as part of our belief system is being used as though it were present-moment truth — *I am smart; I am likeable; I am stupid; I am a loser; I always fail*. If you want to change your life, you will have to consciously reprogram your brain with new present-moment statements and then to take action to reinforce those statements.

Once you take action, it is very hard to dispute your ability to do whatever you've just done, and your belief that you can do it again will grow. Action also stores memory in many places throughout your body, such as in your muscles, which are more difficult to reach with thought alone. As you will read more about later, language-based thought is only a small part of the way our mind communicates with the rest of our body. Action, on the other hand, incorporates a number of sensory-based processes that integrate our mind and body with the rest of the world, so it is a very powerful way to facilitate the process of changing our beliefs.

Choose behaviors that reinforce your new present-moment statement. Plan a set of actions that are consistent with the future belief you are trying to create. Start by looking at your list of details about your new thought. Remember, you won't take action unless you believe it is possible, so choose some actions you think you can take. For example, if people who are valued and worthy human beings invest in their personal development, then a consistent action might be taking a class on personal development, finding a personal development website that you bookmark and visit regularly, or reading a book from a favorite personal-development author.

Use the "Changing a Thought into a Future Expectation" worksheet on the next page (p. 80) to practice the three steps of initiating a new thought, creating details, and taking action.

WORKSHEET: CHANGING A THOUGHT INTO A FUTURE EXPECTATION

New Thought	Details	Actions
Example: *I am a valued and worthy human being.*	1. *A valued and worthy human being communicates love to others.* 2. *A valued and worthy human being respects his or her body.* 3. *A valued and worthy human being feeds his or her mind.*	1. *I will smile at five new people every day.* 2. *I will replace soda with water.* 3. *I can read a book instead of watching TV before going to bed.*
1.	1. 2. 3.	1. 2. 3.
2.	1. 2. 3.	1. 2. 3.
3.	1. 2. 3.	1. 2. 3.
4.	1. 2. 3.	1. 2. 3.

Worksheet 4.3

SEVEN STEPS TO FUTURE SUCCESS

If you have been doing your reading and practicing your assignments, by now you have learned a number of skills that will help you create more positive expectations. When you are feeling down, it can be hard to think clearly and to remember to use your new skills. The seven steps were created to guide you through the process of identifying where you are, figuring out where you want to go, and then turning yourself around and mapping out the steps to get there. Use these steps to guide you through the "Changing Distress into Success" worksheet later in the chapter (p. 84).

Whenever you begin to experience a negative emotion that indicates a negative expectation about the future, you can intercept the process using these seven steps. They involve first becoming aware of what you are feeling and thinking about, then using the process described in this chapter for creating new beliefs.

1. How am I feeling right now? (Emotions are the indicator of thought.)
2. What future event am I thinking of?
3. What unwanted aspect of the situation am I focusing on?
4. What do I really want to have happen in this situation? (Use what you don't want as a guide, and focus on what you control with your thoughts and actions, not on things that are out of your control, such as other people's behavior.)
5. What negative expectations do I have about the situation?
6. What new thoughts can I come up with that move me closer to what I want? Do these thoughts feel like an improvement that I can really buy into, or have I taken too big a leap?
7. What details can I think of and what actions can I take to grow these thoughts into new beliefs?

Let's look at an example that shows how you can take a distressful experience, examine your thoughts and feelings about it using these seven steps, and then make the necessary changes to create a more desired outcome.

Lacy is worried about an upcoming surgery. In the present, she feels fear and anxiety whenever she thinks about it. She is able to recognize from her negative emotions that she is focusing on aspects of the situation that she does not want, so she stops to ask herself what she does want. She is able to identify that what she really wants is to go through the surgery feeling a sense of calm and peace. She knows that her negative feelings of fear and anxiety are coming from the expectation that surgeries cause lots of pain and discomfort. She is anticipating that she will have to experience a great deal of pain after the surgery and need a lot of medication. This adds to her fear and anxiety, because Lacy fought a long battle to overcome addiction to pain medication several years ago, and she fears she will end up addicted again. This particular concern is causing her the fearful anticipation that her family will be angry with her and possibly abandon her.

Lacy knows that to obtain what she wants, which is the feeling of being calm, she is going to have to change her thinking and create a new expectation about the situation. Lacy starts with identifying some thoughts she feels are more in alignment with what she wants, and she writes them down, making sure to phrase them in the present tense. She comes up with *I have doctors I trust and I know my family loves me and wants to be there for me.* Lacy realizes she will need to grow her thoughts and take actions consistent with them if she wants these new thoughts to become real beliefs. So she writes out a list of things she can do that will help grow her new thoughts into real expectations. She decides she will have a conversation with her doctor about nonaddictive pain medication. She also decides to call her family and friends to express her feelings and to ask for their love and support during this difficult time. These actions significantly reduce her fear and anxiety and bring her closer to the sense of peace and calm she is seeking.

Any time you are feeling down and want to turn things around, you too can use the seven steps for future success to help guide you through the "Changing Distress into Success" worksheet. As your behavior starts to align with what you want, you will begin to see yourself differently in the world. Your old, limiting beliefs will no longer seem so true, because you will have created tangible evidence that contradicts them by acting on what you do want. Eventually, those negative beliefs will start to fade away when you no longer reinforce them with actions.

It takes conscious effort, persistence, and courage to choose a new way of thinking, but this process is essential if you want to break free from the past to create a different future.

WORKSHEET: CHANGING DISTRESS INTO SUCCESS

Present:	Future	
Step 1. Indicating emotion (How do I feel right now?) *Scared, fearful, anxious.*	**Step 2.** Projected event: *Upcoming surgery.*	**Step 3.** What unwanted aspect am I focusing on? *It will go badly for me.*
		Step 4. (Point B) What would I like to see happen? *I want to feel calm.*

Point B ⟹

Point B
(Where I want to be)

| **Step 5.**
My negative expectations
about the situation

Point A
(Where I am)

I might feel lots of pain.

*I might get addicted to pain
medication.*

My family will be angry at me. | **Step 6.**
New thoughts to build my future (present tense)
and bring me closer to what I want

I have doctors I trust; my family loves me and wants to be there for me. _____ |
| | **Step 7.**
What details can I think of and what actions can I take to grow my thought into a belief?

1. *I can ask my doctor for nonaddictive pain medication.*

2. *I can tell my family how I am feeling and ask for support.*

3. *I can make a list of people I know support me and call them.* |

From *Think Forward to Thrive* © 2014 by Jennice Vilhauer, PhD

WORKSHEET: CHANGING DISTRESS INTO SUCCESS

Present:	Future	
Step 1. Indicating emotion (How do I feel right now?)	**Step 2.** Projected event:	**Step 3.** What unwanted aspect am I focusing on?
		Step 4. (Point B) What would I like to see happen?

Point B →

Point B
(Where I want to be)

Step 5.
My negative expectations
about the situation

Step 6.
New thoughts to build my future (present tense)
and bring me closer to what I want

Point A
(Where I am) _____

Step 7.
What details can I think of and what actions can I take to grow my thought into a belief?

1.

2.

3.

PRACTICE ASSIGNMENTS

1. As a way to practice thinking your way into a better future, complete the "My New Thoughts about My Future" worksheet on page 77. Identify new thoughts about the different areas of your life, including work, love, play, and perhaps spirituality. Keep in mind that new thoughts should be present-moment statements phrased to imply the presence of things you would like in your life, not the absence of things you don't want.

2. Take your new thoughts and begin turning them into real expectations about the life you desire by completing the "Changing a Thought into a Future Expectation" worksheet on page 80.

3. To practice converting negative emotions about the future into more positive future expectations, use the seven steps to future success to guide you through the process of "Changing Distress into Success" worksheet on page 84.

- When you are thinking about a future experience, your emotions are indicators of what you believe will happen based on past experience. Realize that nothing in the future has actually occurred yet.

- Because we act on what we expect, we create self-fulfilling prophecies. Ask yourself if the expectation you are holding will help you take actions toward what you want, or if you want to create a new experience for yourself by formulating a new future belief. To create a new expectation:

  1. Initiate a new thought about what you would like to see happen in the situation.

  2. Grow the thought as much as possible by imagining what the situation you want would be like and by formulating as many details about it as possible.

  3. Take action, even if it is a small one, consistent with the expectation you want to create.

- When formulating a new way of thinking about the future, keep in mind that you can change only your own thoughts and actions, not those of others.

- When you notice yourself feeling an unwanted emotion about a future situation, pull out your seven steps to future success and the "Changing Distress into Success" worksheet and work your way through the steps until you start to see a change in your thinking and feelings about what you are anticipating.

Chapter 5
OVERCOMING RESISTANCE
TO NEW BELIEFS

When you correct your mind everything else will fall into place.
—LAO TZU

Imagine life as a stream. When you are heading toward thriving, you are flowing with the stream, and things happen with ease. When you are resisting, you are heading upstream, and everything feels difficult. You are not thriving. You want to become sensitive to the ease that comes from flowing with the stream of well-being, so that when you find yourself in a state of resistance, you can turn around.

You can always tell when you are in a state of resistance by how you feel. If you feel contented, peaceful, or optimistic, you are heading downstream with the flow; if you are feeling sad, angry, or anxious, you are probably heading upstream in a state of resistance. Because you already know that thoughts precede feelings, it shouldn't surprise you to learn that your thoughts create the resistance in your life. Resistant thinking creates doubt and keeps you stuck in old patterns of being in the world. As you begin to shift your thinking and to create new beliefs, you may experience doubts and negative thoughts — *I'm not good enough; I'm too old to do this; this will never work* — that get in the way of having what you want.

You can do a number of things to soften the resistance in your thinking. While it may take time for the resistance to dissipate completely, simply being aware of it gives you the opportunity to acknowledge it and make the choice to let it go.

SOFTENING THE RESISTANCE

One reason resistance occurs is that the mind doesn't like taking large leaps in thought. Thoughts tend to occur on a continuum — the farther you try to leap in any direction on the continuum, the more resistance you will encounter. Going from *I hate myself* to *I love myself* is a giant leap. It is much easier to go from *I hate myself* to *I sometimes think I am okay*. Once you have fully transitioned to believing that you are *sometimes okay*, then you can move up the continuum to an even more improved thought, such as *Much of the time, I think I am a pretty decent person*. If you keep moving up the continuum this way, every time you fully begin to accept the new belief, you will eventually reach the point at which you will be able to say, *I love myself completely*.

X   X
| I hate myself. | Sometimes I am okay. | Much of the time I am okay. | I like myself. | I love myself. |

If you are experiencing a negative feeling about your new belief, it most likely means that you have jumped too far up the continuum. Try softening the resistance by reframing the thought in a way that seems like a smaller leap. Look for statements that feel like improvement but are still within the realm of believability. When you have strong patterns of negative thinking, your aim for your new thoughts is to generate feelings along the lines of relief or hope for something better. Use your emotions as the guidance system. When the thought *feels* like something you can buy into, you will have moved into a place of less resistance, and your new belief will have more opportunity to grow.

Take a look at the new thoughts you are working on from the "My New Thoughts about My Future" worksheet on page 77, and see if any of them elicit doubting or resistant thoughts as you read them over. If so, try listing them on the "Identifying Resistance to New Beliefs" worksheet on the next page (p. 89), and see if you can soften the resistance by reframing the thought or stepping it back until it feels like less of a leap.

OTHER WAYS TO OVERCOME RESISTANCE

While resistance almost always comes in the form of negative thoughts that hold you back from forward movement, you can use many different strategies to reduce resistant thinking. Let's take a look at some of them.

FOCUS ON THE FUTURE YOU WANT

Another form of resistance occurs when the present you don't want gets more attention than the future you do want. When you are trying to make a change in your life, a present state exists that is different from the future desired state. In other words, what you have is different from what you want. In the midst of change, the thought process around present states and future intended states can be quite different, and as a result, they each elicit different emotional responses.

WORKSHEET: IDENTIFYING RESISTANCE TO NEW BELIEFS

New Thought	Resistant Thoughts	Softening the Resistance
Example: *I am a valued and worthy human being.*	1. *I've done a lot of bad things in my life.* 2. *No one else thinks I'm worthwhile.* 3. *This is a stupid exercise.*	1. *I've learned from my mistakes.* 2. *What I think about myself is what counts.* 3. *I am willing to try doing something different to get a different result in life.*
1.	1. 2. 3.	1. 2. 3.
2.	1. 2. 3.	1. 2. 3.
3.	1. 2. 3.	1. 2. 3.

From *Think Forward to Thrive* © 2014 by Jennice Vilhauer, PhD

- *I don't have enough time* vs. *I want more time*
- *I feel fat* vs. *I want to be thinner*
- *My house is dirty* vs. *I want a clean house*
- *I don't have a relationship* vs. *I want a great relationship*

Because present states are more real to us than future ones, we much more easily focus our thoughts on what we have or don't have now instead of on what we want. Saying something like, *I feel fat and I want to be thinner* is a good example of this. If you focus on the present-moment reality of I feel fat, you are likely to generate similar thoughts about the subject, such as *Feeling fat is awful; it makes me feel bad about myself; I'm sure other people are thinking bad things about me because I'm fat; no one will ever love me because I'm fat; I ate all that ice cream last night, so I deserve to be fat.* None of these thoughts feel good or help you get closer to what you want; they only make the thing you do want, which is to be thinner, seem further away. You can turn this situation around if you focus instead on the future desired state of *I want to be thinner* and grow your thought process in this direction by imagining what it would be like to be in that future state: *Being thinner would feel great. I would be able to wear my favorite jeans again; I would have more energy, and I would be able to do more of the activities in life I enjoy, like dancing; I would feel more self-confident.*

Remember that thoughts grow. As you grow your thought process around your desired future state, not only do you feel better, but your mind's problem-solving mechanism starts to kick in and generate solutions for how to bring this desired state about. As you will read more about in chapter 10, your mind wants to help you solve problems and prepare for the future as a way to promote your survival. By focusing your thoughts on the future desired state, you start to make it seem more real, and as a result, you generate less resistance to it.

One way to increase thoughts about the future you want is to make that future seem more tangible by exposing yourself to the experience you'd like to have. For example, if you want to go to college but feel stuck in a dead-end job, you can make going to college seem more real by doing activities that expose you to the experience of college, such as spending time in a college library on the weekends, talking to a college counselor, or researching how to pay for college with financial aid. Remember that action leads to belief change. Doing things that expose you to an experience you want to have can increase your belief that it is possible. Other ways to keep your thoughts focused on your desired future state could include finding pictures that represent what you want, then taping them to your refrigerator or gluing them on a poster board, or creating a webpage about your future experience and blogging about the steps you are taking to get there.

There is no right or wrong way; just keep in mind that you want to look for opportunities to spend thought process on what you want. The more time you spend thinking about what you want, the more ideas you will generate about how to make what you want possible. Many of the exercises that follow in this chapter are specifically designed to help you spend more thought on the desired future and make it seem more real.

Eric was having difficulty in his relationship with his wife. He thought she did not understand him and was overly emotional, so he avoided telling her how he felt about many issues in their marriage. He loved his wife and wanted to improve his communication with her, but every time something came up, he would remember situations from the past when he had tried to express himself and it hadn't gone well, and he would shut down. This, of course, created more tension between them, which led him to avoid telling her even small things, like when he would be home. Eric became so focused on the problem in the present and avoiding what he didn't want to experience that he had a hard time imagining what good communication could be like. After discussing his problem in treatment, Eric realized that the only way to create a better relationship with his wife was to keep his attention on his goal. He found a photograph from their wedding, in which they were happy and smiling together, and made it the desktop image on his computer at work. Every time he looked at it, he reminded himself that was how he wanted his relationship with his wife to be, though it seemed like a stark contrast to the way things were now. After a few days of seeing the picture over and over and being reminded of how great things had been when they first met, Eric decided to take a risk and, with some hesitation, initiated a discussion about couples counseling with his wife. They began working with a professional to improve their communication skills.

SAVOR THE PROGRESS

Many people, when they start to focus on their wanted future, get stuck when they let their minds drift back toward the realization that they have not yet arrived. This can cause distress, since they are *resisting* instead of embracing the journey. No matter how much you want to arrive, there is always travel distance; how much depends on where you start. If you believe you cannot be happy until you arrive, you will always be unhappy knowing you are not there. The main problem with this type of thinking is that every time you arrive somewhere you will find there is somewhere else to go. You will live in the pursuit of happiness without realizing that happiness is in the pursuit.

As you know, we feel a sense of thriving when we believe we are making forward progress toward our growth and expansion. However, in order to experience this sense of thriving you must actually notice that forward movement and growth are occurring. When all your attention is focused on the fact that you have not yet arrived, you will have difficulty seeing how far you have come. Take credit for your progress on the journey, because each step forward is necessary. The steps forward are what help us to grow.

Most of us do not start out prepared to achieve the goals we set for ourselves. If you want to run a marathon, you have to train to prepare yourself for success. If you never exercise and then you decide to enter a marathon, chances are you would never make it, and you could even hurt yourself trying. Similarly, you wouldn't want to go to a "doctor" who decided to skip the eight years of required medical education. You would want to go to someone who trained and gained the experience needed to become a medical expert. It is the journey toward our goals that prepares us for who we will be when we finally arrive. Many of the obstacles and failures that we encounter along the way can be opportunities for learning.

Be proud of every step you take forward; you are one step closer than you were before. Don't just acknowledge the progress; really savor it, because doing so builds positive thought and emotion, which will only aid you further. Conversely, if you don't acknowledge your progress and you focus only on not having yet arrived, not only do you miss the opportunity to benefit from all you've done, but you also increase negative emotions and create resistance, which inhibits you from building forward momentum and, indeed, slows you down.

One way to savor your progress is to simply write down the steps you've taken toward your goal at the end of each day or at least once a week. They don't have to be huge steps. Something such as *Today I bought a book on how to*...is a step in the right direction and something to feel good about. As you keep track of your progress, you will have compiled a tangible record to focus on, one that documents all the accomplishments you have made so far.

If you believe you cannot be happy until you arrive,
you will always be unhappy knowing you are not there.

TELL A DIFFERENT STORY

You tell the story of your life every day. You talk about it with your family, friends, and coworkers all the time. You share your experiences as a way to be heard and validated, to seek advice or support. Sharing helps us to connect with others and usually makes us feel good. But have you ever stopped to think about the fact that there may be a downside to telling the story of your life in its current form? What if you don't like your life? What if the stories you tell all day are about people, things, or events that bring on negative emotions such as anger, hurt, or sadness? What if the validation you are getting from others only reinforces your negative perspective? Does telling these stories help you generate any ideas about how to improve your situation and get what you want?

While we tell our stories to other people for many different reasons, the way we tell these stories can have a profound impact on whether the result of our having shared ultimately moves us closer to or further from where we want to go. When you tell a story about some troubling event, you grow your thoughts about the unwanted situation. When you add someone else to the mix, you run the risk of adding *their* thoughts about what you don't want to the situation as well. Most of the people you tell your stories to will try to offer their support for your perspective. It is the socially acceptable thing to do. It is a rare friend who will dare to tell you that your thinking may be wrong. If you'd like to get support for the things you desire, you need to start including those things in your stories; learn to tell your stories in a way that indicates hope for something better.

Here is an example of what can happen if you change a story that focuses on the unwanted present to one that includes hope about your desired future:

Old Story (about the present)
Friend: How are you?
You: Lousy! My boyfriend is such a jerk. He never listens to me. We had a huge argument last night because I had to ask him five times to take out the trash.
Friend: That's too bad. You're right, he sounds like a total jerk.
You: Isn't he, though? I'm glad you agree. I'm going to tell him everyone I know agrees with me. Do you think I should leave him?
Friend: If I were you I would leave him. A guy that acts like a jerk doesn't deserve you.

New Story (about the present but including what you want in the future)
Friend: How are you?
You: Mmm, last night was tough because my boyfriend and I had an argument, but I thought it through and realized I can try harder to communicate with him, so I think things are going to get better.

Friend: That's great. You must really like him if you are willing to work that hard on the relationship.

You: Well, sometimes he acts like a jerk, but I also realize he has a lot of good qualities, and I am going to focus on those parts of him because I love him and would like the relationship to work.

Friend: If he makes you feel that way, he must be pretty special.

Telling a story about what you want (better communication with your boyfriend) instead of what you don't want (a jerk for a boyfriend) doesn't mean you can't speak your truth. If you're having a lousy day, you don't have to lie and say you are having a great day just because that is what you want to be having. You can state your truth — just don't stop there. Finish with creating hope for something better. For example, *I'm having a lousy day, but I am looking forward to going home to enjoy a nice, relaxing evening, and I plan to have a much better day tomorrow.*

Tell a story about what you want as the outcome. When you do, you generate thoughts about the presence of what you would like to create in your future. By activating a thought process around what you want, you plant the seeds for this thought to grow into something more. Doing so will increase your belief that it is possible and, therefore, increase the likelihood you will take actions to make it happen. And if you tell people what you want instead of what you don't want, you will also be creating opportunities for gaining more support. The next time you are talking with someone, ask yourself:

ASK YOURSELF

Am I telling a story about what I want or what I don't want?

WHAT'S YOUR STORY? When asked this question, most people immediately think about everything that has happened to them in the past. In particular, they seem to think of all the painful or difficult things they have been through. Rarely do they think about where they are going. But where you are going is far more important than where you've been. If you want to create your future by choice instead of by default, you will need to map out a story of where you want to go. The more you start to think about the story of where you are going, the more vivid and detailed it will become as you grow more thought around it. If it seems artificial to tell a story about things you haven't done yet, then tell the story in terms of what you value and aspire to in life.

Where you are going is far more important than where you've been.

WORKSHEET: THE STORY OF MY FUTURE LIFE

Create a future-oriented story about your life. Write the story in the present tense, using *presence of* statements. (If you don't remember what those are, review the section about initiating a new thought in chapter 4.) If it seems strange to write a story about your future in the present tense, you can phrase it this way: *In the future I am successful*—which is more powerful than saying *I will become successful someday.* When you are done, remove the words *In the future*, and you will have a future story of your life written in the present tense. Repeat this story to yourself and everyone else you know as frequently as you can.

HAVE A CONVERSATION WITH YOUR FUTURE SELF

As we've discussed, the more real the future seems, the less resistance you will have to it. It probably feels very real that you will go to bed tonight and wake up tomorrow morning, so you don't have much resistance to that thought. However, the idea that one day you might be a millionaire probably seems hard to believe, so trying to imagine what it would feel like creates internal resistance and elicits doubts.

Now that you have imagined the future story of your life, to grow your thought process about it, you must begin to really see yourself in the story. One effective way to make your future seem more real is to get to know your future self as well as possible and then to ask your present self to have a conversation with your desired future self.

To have a conversation with your future self, you will have to activate a good deal of imagination about your desired future. This is a good thing, because you want your brain working as hard as possible on creating your new experience. Use the following questions to begin creating a mental image: Where is your future self? What does your future self look like? What is your future self doing? What is your future self thinking? What is your future self feeling? Don't hesitate to imagine as many details as you can about your future self, such as what he or she eats for lunch.

Once you have created the mental image of your future self, imagine your present self having a conversation with your future self. Be creative. You can talk about anything you want, but remember, the goal is to get into the mind-set of your future self, so don't forget to ask the important questions. Here are a few examples to start with:

- *What does it feel like being here (in the future)?*
- *Is the journey worth it?*
- *What advice do you have for me?*
- *What is the best part about being here?*
- *What was the most difficult challenge in getting here?*
- *How did you overcome that challenge?*

Keep this image of your future self in your mind and talk to him or her any time you are feel sad or anxious because you are overly focused on a present undesired state. Use your conversations with your future self as a way to turn yourself around so that you can again start moving toward your natural state of thriving.

ENTRENCHED RESISTANCE: INEFFECTIVE THOUGHT PATTERNS

There is an old saying in the field of psychology: *If something happens once, it is an incident; if it happens twice, it is a coincidence; if it happens three times, it's a pattern.* Many people go through life wondering why the same unwanted things keep happening to them. What psychologists know from many years of studying human thought process is that human beings are capable of continually applying ineffective patterns of thinking without realizing they are doing so. The thought patterns are so over-learned that they become schemas, or filters through which we view the world and interpret the things that happen to us. Most people believe that their patterns of thinking are simply the "truth" of how the world operates. The problem is that when you apply the same ineffective patterns of thinking over and over again, it is like playing the game of life with the wrong rules. You never come out the winner.

We remain entrenched in thought patterns that aren't working and that create resistance to future goals for several reasons. One reason is that we may have been taught to think unproductive thoughts by other people, such as our parents, who were also thinking ineffectively. In essence, incorrect thinking can be passed on from one generation to the next. Another reason is that thought patterns may be reinforced by other people who share the same patterns of thought within our family or culture. In other words, when you think a certain way, other people around you may agree with you and tell you that your way of thinking is correct. For example, some cultures teach people that they should not say no to others. If never saying no works, then there is nothing wrong with thinking that way, but if it is causing you distress, then holding on to that pattern of thought is ineffective at best and destructive at worst.

Many recurring negative emotions are the result of an ineffective thought pattern. Disappointment, anger, resentment, and deep hurt often stem from viewing the world and other people through a distorted lens. You find yourself constantly trying to make the world fit your way of thinking, which leads to endless frustration, because you don't recognize that your way of thinking is not necessarily an accurate view of how the world works.

Becoming aware of ineffective thought patterns is essential to changing how you think about the future. As you begin to recognize your thought patterns, you will begin to shift your view of who you are in the world and where the power over your life lies. Initially, some people are resistant to letting go of their old patterns of thinking because admitting how they've always thought might not be entirely correct can feel very threatening. Below is a discussion of several common patterns of ineffective thinking; as you review them, keep an open mind and remember that the purpose of identifying these patterns is to free you from a way of thinking that is keeping you from developing a better future.

I SHOULD BE SOMEWHERE ELSE

You can only be where you are. Many people waste endless energy and thoughts making themselves unhappy by believing that they should be somewhere other than where they are: *I should have gone to school; I should have a fancy car and house by now; I should be married with kids at this age; I should be thinner.* This belief that you should be somewhere else generally stems from comparing yourself to other people — seeing where they are and believing that somehow you should be there too. This is an ineffective thought pattern because comparing yourself to someone else does not take into account the fact that you have had completely different life experiences. Even if you had exactly the same life experiences as someone else (which isn't possible), you were born with different genetic makeups and, therefore, would have different responses to events in your lives. Essentially, people do not all come out of the same starting gate; therefore, head-to-head competition with others does not make sense. It only keeps you from taking credit for what you have achieved based on your own set of circumstances.

Your life experience is your own. Everything is as it should be based on what you have learned and what you were given in life in terms of biology and experiences. If you really could be somewhere else, don't you think you would be? At any given moment, given our circumstances, we make the best choices we can about what we believe will help us thrive. Even when you know in advance that you will regret a choice, at the time it feels like the thing to do; otherwise, you wouldn't choose to do it. If you were in a position to overcome your fear or access the power inside you and make a choice that you knew in the long run was better for you, you would. The truth is that you don't do it because you simply aren't there yet.

Keep in mind that you can only look back because of how far you've come. The fact that you have enough insight to recognize an alternative shows that you have already grown beyond where you were at the time you made your decision. I will say it again: wherever you are in your journey of becoming who you want to be is simply where you are. This observation isn't an excuse to maintain the status quo; rather, the goal is to always keep reaching forward to close the gap between where you are and where you want to be. Doing so is the very definition of thriving. But do realize that getting to where you want to be is a process, and beating yourself up because you're not there already is a waste of precious resources. Instead, ask yourself what you can learn from the situations in the past or present that may bring you closer to what you are hoping for in the future. If your life is not what you want it to be, there are still so many things for you to achieve, and you are in the process of learning how to obtain more of what you desire. Accepting that where you are is the only place you can be at the moment will allow you to spend more of your energy and thoughts on where you are going.

I Can't Be Happy until My Environment and the People in It Change

Your happiness is determined by what you think. As we've seen, our emotions are determined by what we think and believe. Allowing your emotions to fluctuate with the events of the environment is referred to as *regulating to the external*. Most people do not consciously attend to their thought process, so they allow their emotional states to fluctuate based on whatever is going on. As a result, they often believe that what is happening outside them is *causing* them to feel a certain way. In fact, you have the power to maintain any emotional state you choose, regardless of what is happening outside you, by changing how you think about the situation. If you find yourself thinking that something in your environment must change in order for you to feel happy, take a step back and see if you can instead change how you are thinking about the situation.

Having a preference for one environment over the other does not mean your environment is determining your emotions. You can prefer sunny days but still be happy when it rains. Remember that formulating preferences is a normal part of how we function and helps us determine what we want. As you will learn in chapter 7, however, knowing that your emotional well-being is not dependent on realizing every preference gives you much more control over your life.

One of the most common areas in which people regulate to the external is in their relationships with others. If you presume that how you feel is dependent on how other people behave, you have relinquished all control over your well-being to people over whom you have no control. And yet we do this all the time. Here are some examples of this type of thinking:

- If my sister apologized to me I would stop being angry.
- If my husband would just be more romantic I would feel more content in the relationship.
- If my kids would pick better friends I could stop worrying about them all the time.
- If my neighbors would stop playing their music so loudly I wouldn't have to get so upset.
- If my friend would call me more often I would feel happier, because then I would know she values my friendship.

Believing that your happiness depends on someone else almost always results in frustration and unhappiness. If you have to wait for other people to change before you can be happy, you ride the wave of other people's whims. Additionally, you may generate resentment from others who do not feel it is their job to please you.

WHAT OTHER PEOPLE THINK IS MORE IMPORTANT THAN MY OWN OPINION

Your opinion of you matters most. We all love validation. When someone pays us a compliment, it feels great. When someone apologizes, it feels good, because it validates our perspective. We were right, he was wrong, and he has agreed to accept our view. Because it feels so good to be validated by other people, other people's opinions of us often become more important than the opinions we have of ourselves. However, trying to make everyone else happy by changing who you are or what you do is a losing battle. You will eventually run into those who can't be pleased, or you will find that pleasing one person ends up displeasing someone else.

What matters most is that you learn to value your own opinion of who you are and what you do. This is not the same as being narcissistic. Narcissism stems from underlying insecurity and often involves seeing oneself as better than others. Liking who you are means that you assign yourself and others equal value; it doesn't mean that you disrespect or devalue someone else.

When you value yourself, you do not spend your time trying to become what someone else wants you to be but rather what *you* want to be. We are all born with an internal instinct that tells us when what we are doing is in our own best interests. If you listen, this instinct will guide you. If you grew up in an invalidating environment in which you learned to doubt yourself and your inner voice, you may have to work a bit harder to tune back in to it. However, your internal instinct, which points you in the direction of thriving, is always present.

You might find yourself in situations that have an inherent power difference, such as an employer-employee relationship in which your boss's opinion of you does matter if you want to keep your job. But this does not mean that your boss's opinion is more important than yours. Your boss may tell you that you are a worthless human being every day, but that doesn't make it so. That is his or her opinion, and you are choosing to endure that opinion so that you can keep your job and earn an income. In other words, while other people's approval may provide us with the opportunity to obtain something we want, that doesn't mean their opinion is inherently more valuable than our opinion of ourselves.

Valuing yourself as central to the process of creating your future is about recognizing a very simple premise — that your experience in the world starts with you. We've discussed the concept of a self-fulfilling prophecy; when you feel good about who you are, you will create a self-fulfilling prophecy of success, since your beliefs and actions will generate experiences that you feel good about. When you do what is truly right for you and take care of yourself, the people who care about you will be happy for you. Those who only care about what you do to make them happy are probably not worth having around.

THE WORLD IS DIVIDED INTO GOOD AND BAD AND RIGHT AND WRONG

There is no universal right or wrong way to think about anything. The world is made up of many shades of gray. While many people may agree with your way of thinking, that doesn't make it universally applicable to all people. Some people believe that killing someone is always wrong, while others believe that it is the path to religious righteousness. Some believe it is permissible to kill someone who has done wrong to others in society or who is threatening others' safety and well-being. How you think about an event determines how you feel about it. The guide to what is right or wrong for you personally is whether or not your actions lead you to feel better or worse about who you are and where you are going.

Believing there is one right or wrong way to live leads to many kinds of difficulties, such as perfectionism, which can seriously impair progress toward your future. It can stop you from taking action, because you fear doing something incorrectly. When you are working so hard to be perfect that it is keeping you from moving forward, it is because you are spending too much of your thought process on the thing you *don't want*, which is "doing it wrong." To get past this, redirect your thinking toward what you do want, which is to accomplish your task, and spend more of your thoughts on all the reasons you want to accomplish it. Remember, there is no such thing as perfect, and trying is the purpose of life. Success comes from trying, no matter how many times you fail. When you try, you open yourself up to the possibility of learning and experiencing something new, and give yourself the opportunity to create something different.

The idea that there is no right or wrong way to think may be difficult for many to accept. All conflict results from one person believing that another person should change. While it is nice when people do things that please us or that accord with our point of view, other people have the right to be who they are, just as you have a right to be who you are. You can learn to observe any event, including the actions of others, in a nonjudgmental way, as we'll discuss in a later chapter. When you remove the labels of good and bad, right and wrong, you free yourself from the emotional impact of situations that are usually out of your control. Determine that you will focus on what you can control, regardless of what others choose to do, and learn to respect the right of others to be who they are.

Rachael was a hospital administrator in her midfifties who for most of her life had very entrenched patterns of ineffective thought. She felt deep unhappiness and resentment toward the people in her life who she felt did not live up to her standards. If someone did not return a phone call when she expected him to or behaved in some way she found unacceptable, she could become quite upset and angry, often deciding to end relationships with people over small misunderstandings. At the same time, however, Rachael often felt lonely and as if she didn't have many friends. She wondered why she couldn't meet quality people. What Rachael didn't realize was that she was making her happiness dependent on the behavior of others in a rigid way. She was taking small things personally and expecting everyone in her life to conform to her beliefs about how they should behave. Rachael realized that she did not want her sense of happiness to be dependent on others' behavior, and she decided to take responsibility for her own happiness by focusing more on herself. When she did, she noticed that other people's behavior started to upset her far less. When one of her friends forgot to call her on her birthday but called the next day to apologize, Rachael was surprised that she wasn't bothered much by it, and she easily forgave her friend's forgetfulness.

CREATING EFFECTIVE THOUGHT PATTERNS

The list we've just gone through is a brief summary of some common ineffective thought patterns. What matters most is that you begin to identify the patterns that are relevant to you, because your thought patterns are what you use to appraise your life and build your future. If you aren't feeling good about a situation, take a look at the primary emotion the situation is generating and see if similar situations have happened before that generated similar feelings. Use the following four principles of emotionally effective thought (see next page) as a guide to exploring your thought patterns. If your thought patterns are not aligning with these principles, chances are they are ineffective patterns that may have been reinforced at some point but are unlikely to represent how the world really works. More important, they are likely contributing to your negative emotions and creating resistance to the future life you are trying to achieve.

The Four Principles of Emotionally Effective Thought	Ask Yourself
1. You can only be where you are at any given moment.	• *Am I upset because I feel like I should be somewhere else?*
2. Your happiness is determined by what you think, not by your environment or the people in it.	• *Am I blaming my environment for how I feel?* • *Am I blaming someone else for how I feel?* • *Do I think my environment must change before I can feel better?*
3. Your opinion of yourself matters most.	• *Am I worrying too much about what other people think?* • *Am I listening to my own instinct?*
4. There is no universal right or wrong.	• *Am I assuming there is a right or wrong answer or position?* • *Am I expecting someone else to take my view of the world?*

From *Think Forward to Thrive* © 2014 by Jennice Vilhauer, PhD

WORKSHEET: CREATING EFFECTIVE PATTERNS OF THOUGHT

Event	Emotionally Ineffective Thought	Emotionally Effective Principle	New Thought
Example: *My best friend canceled our plans at the last minute.*	*I can't believe how wrong that was. I will feel upset unless she apologizes.*	*My happiness is determined by what I think, not by my environment or the people in it.*	*It would be nice if she apologized, but if she doesn't, I can still feel good about myself and not be angry.*
1.			
2.			
3.			
4.			

Worksheet 5.3

Practice Assignments

1. Complete the worksheet "Identifying Resistance to New Beliefs" worksheet on page 89.

2. Start thinking about the story of your future instead of the story of your past. Write down what you would like the story of your future to be on page 95, so that when someone asks, "What's your story?" you can tell her about where you're going instead of where you've been.

3. Once you've written the story of your future self, reread the section on having a conversation with your future self. Really imagine yourself in the story, and bring it to life.

4. Examine the situations in your life that are causing you distress. Use the "Creating Effective Patterns of Thought" worksheet on page 104 to record your thinking about them and see if there is an emotionally effective thought principle you can apply to formulate a new, more productive thought.

Tips for Thriving

- When you make big leaps in thought, your mind will produce resistance. To minimize resistance, instead of making a big leap, reach for a new thought that represents improvement but still feels believable.

- Many people resist change by spending most of their thought process on the present moment, where they don't want to be, instead of on a future place where they do want to be. Spend as much of your thought process as you can on the future to make it real and tangible.

- In our day-to-day communications with people we all tell stories; however, the story of what is happening in the present might not be helping you to create a better future. Instead of only telling the story of now, begin to tell stories that indicate your hope for something better.

- Remember, where you are going is far more important than where you have been. Repeat the story of your future life to as many people as possible. Tell people where you are going!

- To make your future seem more real, and to spend more thought on your future, have a conversation with your future self.

- Human beings are capable of applying ineffective patterns of thinking without realizing that they are doing it. These thought patterns can keep you stuck in an entrenched way of doing things that prevents you from building a better future. Remember the four principles of emotionally effective thought:

  1. You can only be where you are at any given moment.
  2. Your happiness is determined by what you think, not by your environment or the people in it.
  3. Your opinion of yourself matters most.
  4. There is no universal right or wrong.

Chapter 6

MINDFULNESS AND MEDITATION

The future depends on what we do in the present.
—MAHATMA GANDHI

By now we know well that the present moment is where we create the future. Being aware of your thoughts and actions right now is essential because the choices you make in each moment build the next present moment that you experience. Learning how to redirect your thinking and to spend more of your thought process on what you want depends on present-moment awareness. Mindfulness and meditation are two skills that will help you become more aware of your present experience so that you can make active choices about the future you're creating.

THE CONSCIOUS OBSERVER

You may have heard the famous expression "I think, therefore I am." This statement by René Descartes was held as the truth for many years, until Jean-Paul Sartre argued that thought begins with the human subject, the "I am." This "I am" is the level of consciousness that exists in all human beings, allowing us to observe our own thoughts.

Most people believe they *are* their thought process. The majority of our thoughts, however, are our interpretations of our environment, based on past experience and future expectation. We can change our interpretations depending on what perspective we take, and while the events in your past (and many in your present) cannot be changed, the lens through which you observe those events can change. When you become mindfully aware of your thought process, you are more able to observe it and make choices about the lens through which you view your life. Being mindful allows you to direct your attention to any aspect of a situation you choose; it gives you the power to shift from focusing on what is unwanted to what is wanted in life, thus altering your experience.

Many people come to identify themselves with their experiences. *I am an abused child, I am an alcoholic, I am a lawyer, I am a depressed person.* But these are your roles and experiences, not who you are. Much like an actor in a movie or play, you can assume a role at any time, but you can also stop playing that role if you decide to. Harrison Ford can stop being Indiana Jones and be Harrison Ford again. You are not stuck with a defined identity based on your history. Until you realize this, you will continue to create your future based on the roles and experiences that you believe define who you are.

Who you really are is a conscious, creative being, continuously in the process of becoming. Imagine a beautiful flowing stream. Now imagine a rock in the stream. The same water will never pass over the rock twice. The water that flowed over the rock in one moment is being carried farther and farther away from the rock with every moment that passes. You are like the water in the stream, and the rock is like an event in your life. You are not any of those events, nor are you any of the roles you played during those events. With every passing moment you become someone different, moving farther away from events in the past and toward the future you are creating.

You have the ability to observe your thoughts and experiences, and you can watch them from any distance you choose, just like being in a movie theater. You can sit in the front row, or you can watch from way in the back. If you sit too close up, you may not be able to see the whole screen, and parts of it may seem fuzzy. The farther back you sit, the more you will be able to see the whole picture — not just what is happening on the screen but everything going on around it as well. You will see the boy eating popcorn and the lovers holding hands as well as the drama taking place on the movie screen.

Without realizing it, many people are sitting in the front row, so close to their thoughts and experiences that they feel enmeshed with them and believe them to be the entirety of who they are. They don't have a full perspective on what they think or experience; they have a thought or a feeling but they don't know where it comes from, so they often feel confused and uncertain. If you step back and observe more, you will become more aware of what is unfolding all around you. When you can see the whole picture, you can make better and more meaningful choices. The paradox is that you can engage more fully in life if you first disengage from it enough to step back and see what is truly going on.

Learning to observe nonjudgmentally is the key to distancing yourself just far enough to see the whole picture. Mindfulness and meditation are two ways to get that distance, by increasing your ability to observe your thoughts and experiences so that you can make more informed choices.

You can engage more fully in life if you first disengage
enough to step back and see what is truly going on.

HOW MINDFULNESS AND MEDITATION
CAN HELP CREATE YOUR FUTURE

All the skills you are learning in this book require present-moment awareness to put them into action. You must be aware of your old beliefs, and decide whether to keep them or to create a new expectation that brings you closer to your desired outcome. Without awareness of your thoughts and emotions in the present moment, you cannot change. Realize, however, that mindfulness is about awareness more than it is about any given time frame. You can mindfully think of the past, the present, or the future. Being mindful is about having full awareness of what you are thinking and experiencing in the present, no matter what time frame you are thinking about. If you are thinking about a future event that makes you anxious, you want to mindfully be aware that this is because you are focused on an unwanted aspect of the situation, so that you can mindfully choose to have a new expectation and mindfully engage in different actions.

One of the greatest benefits to these practices is that they help you become more aware of what is happening in the present, which includes noticing what you are thinking about, and only if you are aware of it can you change it. Once you have trained your mind to observe and focus, you will have much more ability to direct your thought process and, subsequently, control your emotions. Another very valuable function of meditation and mindfulness is that they help us stop our negative thought stream. People who often feel anxious or depressed have an automatic tendency to focus on the unwanted aspects of life, which results in a lot of negative internal dialogue that moves them away from thriving. By staying in the present moment and focusing on something specific that is desirable, you will automatically be taking your attention away from unwanted situations that are making you unhappy or anxious. We've talked about the need to slow our thoughts down when they are racing in the wrong direction. Mindfulness is one of the best slow-down techniques there is, and it can help you turn your thoughts around and head them in the direction you want them to go. Since thoughts affect our mood, simply stopping a negative thought flow, even if only for a few minutes, can do us a lot of good.

What Mindfulness and Meditation Are Not

The two most common misconceptions about mindfulness and meditation are:

1. **These are religious practices.** While mindfulness and meditation are practices used in many Eastern religions, you do not need to have a religious affiliation or beliefs of any kind to practice the techniques. The techniques themselves have been used widely in many evidence-based forms of cognitive psychology, and they have been shown to be effective ways of gaining more awareness of your thought process.
2. **These are just relaxation techniques.** While mindfulness and meditation can be relaxing, these techniques have the specific intent of helping you gain greater awareness and control over your thought process. There are many forms of relaxation that involve neither mindfulness nor meditation.

Now let's talk about what mindfulness and mediation are. We'll start with mindfulness.

Mindfulness

Mindfulness is the practice of being fully aware of what is happening in the present moment. It involves being aware of each thought, feeling, and sensation that arises. When you concentrate all your senses and energy on the present, you will be able to experience your environment with much greater clarity, and often you will observe things you might never have noticed otherwise. Our attention is often divided by the many thoughts running through our heads. For example, simply driving home on the freeway can become a very busy task: you are paying attention to traffic while listening to the radio and singing along to your favorite lyrics, thinking about your coworker who gave you a dirty look, wondering what you will make for dinner and whether you need to go to the grocery store and what else you might need while you're there. All of a sudden you're at your exit and you don't even remember how you got there — or maybe you drive past the exit altogether. A mindful drive home would involve being fully aware of and thinking only about what is happening with every present moment of the drive. You are paying attention to the way the steering wheel feels in your hand and the feel of the seat supporting your body, feeling yourself breathe, smelling the burning rubber of the truck next to you, feeling your stomach grumbling, and observing the color of the flowers on the side of the highway.

Another key component of mindfulness is not passing judgment about what is happening. We often observe something in our environment and, without even being aware of it, immediately make a judgment. *That looks like a boring book, that man's tie is ugly, this food tastes terrible, my thighs look fat in these pants, they are a really odd couple, when I say that I sound stupid.* Having preferences for things is natural and helps us discern what we want and what is good for us. However, without even realizing it, many of us train ourselves to make critical or negative judgments in a way that leaves us feeling bad and limits our experience. Preference is about what we like; judgment tends to be about labeling what we don't like as wrong. *I like red; the color orange is awful.* As we know, there is no right or wrong way to think about anything. Some people find orange a lovely color. When you can observe what is happening in both your internal and external environment in a nonjudgmental way, you also develop an attitude of curiosity, openness, tolerance, and acceptance toward your world.

Preference is about what we like; judgment tends to be about labeling what we don't like as wrong.

BECOMING MINDFUL

You can be mindful anywhere and anytime, no matter what you are doing or thinking about. You simply have to draw your attention to the present moment and observe what is happening. Most people find that this takes considerable practice, and many combine mindfulness with meditation to build basic how-to skills. Below are a few simple exercises for you to try yourself. If you find your mind wandering during the exercises, simply notice your thoughts without judgment and bring them back to the exercise.

MINDFUL BREATHING

1. To start, find a comfortable place to sit, preferably one that allows you to keep your back straight.
2. Next, find the breath. You are looking for the actual physical sensation of the breath passing in and out of your nose. If you prefer, you can focus instead on the expansion and contraction of your chest or belly as you inhale and exhale.
3. Once you find the breath, take one deep breath and hold both the inhale and the exhale for one long count. Keep going until you get to ten, and

then start over. Try to keep going for at least five rounds of ten. If you prefer, you can simply say to yourself "I am breathing in" as you inhale and "I am breathing out" as you exhale.

4. Notice all the sensations associated with the breath. Notice how it moves in and out of your body. Notice your chest and ribs expanding and contracting. Notice the air passing across your upper lip. Notice any other physical sensations you become aware of.

MINDFUL SITTING

No matter where you are sitting, you can become aware of the angles of your sitting posture.

1. Begin by planting your feet on the floor and noticing the feeling of your feet meeting the floor.
2. Wiggle your toes and flex your feet one time up and down.
3. Now move your attention to your ankles and slowly up your shins to your knees. Notice how your knees bend at a 90-degree angle.
4. Now slowly bring your attention up your thighs to your hips. Focus on your hips for a minute. They should be the cornerstone of the sitting posture, with the majority of your weight distributed over them. Notice the weight there.
5. Now move your attention slowly from your hips to the base of your spine.
6. Slowly move your attention up your spine, one vertebra at a time. Notice the point in your spine where it curves.
7. As you reach your shoulder blades, notice how they feel. Are they tense or relaxed? Take a deep breath, and notice your shoulders rising up and down.
8. Now move your attention to your neck, then slowly up your neck to the base of your skull. Pause for a moment and notice the distinction between your skull and neck.
9. Now move your attention slowly over your skull, coming down across your forehead and resting at the spot at the center between your eyes.
10. See if you can hold your attention there for a few minutes. If your mind wanders, return to your feet and repeat the process.

MINDFUL LISTENING

At every moment of the day there are noises all around you, many of which you don't even notice. The sounds probably come in layers. Some are nearby, some are distant; they may be loud or very faint.

1. To begin mindful listening, close your eyes and simply listen.
2. See how many sounds you can identify.
3. Savor each sound as you notice it, as if it were something delicious to eat.
4. Pick one sound to focus on and see what details you notice about it. Dissect the various components of the sound. Is there a cadence? Does it stop and start? Are there any layers to the sound that you didn't notice originally?
5. Move to another sound and repeat the process.

MEDITATION

Meditation is the practice of focusing your thought process, most often for the purpose of introspection and attaining greater internal awareness. Through meditation you learn to determine where your attention goes. Meditation sharpens your concentration and your ability to think. People often complain that meditation is difficult for them because stopping thought seems impossible. The goal should not be to *stop* thought, but rather to learn to *focus* your thoughts. As you become adept at focusing your mind on things you want, the other, unwanted thoughts will automatically taper off. Until then, noticing your thoughts wandering and then bringing your attention back to whatever you are focusing on is simply a part of the training process.

WORD FOCUS MEDITATION

One way to reduce the onset of intrusive thoughts is through active meditation, which engages multiple mental processes in a focused way. Your brain has a limited attentional capacity, meaning it has the power to consciously focus on a limited number of things at one time. The more focused tasks you give your brain to do, the less room there will be for intrusive thoughts.

Try the following active meditation to improve your ability to focus your thought process.

1. Pick one word from the list below that describes an emotion you would like to feel more of:

    Joy, Love, Happy, Peace, Calm, Hope
2. Close your eyes and visualize that word in your head.
3. Pick a color that goes with the word, and visualize the word in that color.
4. Fill in the background with another color.
5. Now, writing in your head, inscribe the word in cursive one letter at a time.

6. As you are writing the word, say the letters quietly to yourself in your head.

7. Write the colored word on the colored background over and over in your head while you say the letters quietly to yourself. Do this for five minutes every morning when you wake up and for five minutes every evening before you go to sleep.

8. If your mind wanders or thoughts still intrude, simply acknowledge the thoughts without judgment and move back to the exercise until you have completed it.

BREATHING MEDITATION

One of the simplest forms of meditation is a breathing meditation in which you focus only on your breath. To get started, find a place to sit, again preferably with your back straight. You can do meditation lying down, but when you first start out with this practice, you run the risk of falling asleep.

Since the goal here is to focus on your breath, find one spot in your body where you can feel the breath and focus your attention there. The easiest way to do this is to close your eyes, take a deep breath, and exhale quickly until you feel the air leaving your nose and flowing across your upper lip. You want to find the point where you feel the air leaving your nose and focus on that point. Focus on the natural and spontaneous movement of the breath; don't try to control or regulate it in any way. Let the breath flow naturally, in its own rhythm, as if you were asleep. The goal of the meditation is to focus your attention on breathing; however, when you start out, your focus may not be strong enough to prevent you from getting lost in your thoughts. In this case, counting may be helpful as a way to train the focus on the breath. There is no right way to count, but it should be systematic. Below are a few simple examples of counting you can do while breathing.

*   While inhaling count one, while exhaling count two, inhale and count three, exhale and count four. Keep going until you get to ten, then start over.
*   Count each inhale and exhale together as one number. This is a slower and more relaxed count.
*   Count up to three — one, two, three — as you inhale and one, two, three as you exhale. Keep repeating.

Keep in mind that the goal of meditating and being mindful, from the perspective of FDT, is to gain awareness of your thoughts and the choices you are making in the present that create your future experiences. The goal is to consciously direct your attention in the present moment so that you can focus on what you want. Mastering this skill will change your life. There are many other benefits to mindfulness and meditation that you may wish to explore further on your own. Also, the exercises presented in this chapter are designed for beginners, so as you master these skills you may wish to advance your practice by going to a meditation center or taking a course on mindfulness. There are many books written on the subject that can enhance your knowledge and skills in these areas as well. A simple internet search will provide you with an abundance of resources and information on these topics.

Andy thought people who meditated were weirdos. He just wasn't into that kind of thing, so even getting him to close his eyes and take a deep breath was a challenge. He said it felt strange and unnatural. So Andy was given the task of keeping his eyes open and counting the number of times he saw his stomach rise and fall as he breathed during a two-minute period. After two minutes, Andy said he had been so preoccupied with counting that he had forgotten about the upsetting fight he'd had with his father earlier that day. He admitted to recognizing that keeping thought focused in the present was a good way to turn off negative streams of thought. He agreed to try the exercise at home when he was feeling anxious, and he reported in his next session that it had seemed like a useful tool to help him calm down at several tense moments. After a week Andy agreed to try a meditation CD for fifteen minutes a day. He was surprised that the calm he experienced while listening to the CD seemed to stay with him throughout the day.

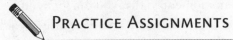

PRACTICE ASSIGNMENTS

Only those who meditate regularly can judge whether or not it is worthwhile. Remember, meditation and mindfulness are learned skills in the same way that playing the piano is a learned skill. That means that in order to improve, you need steady, consistent practice. If you only practice the piano once in a while, chances are you will never become good at it. To become good at being mindful and to reap the benefits of being more aware of your thought process, you must practice regularly.

1. Do one of the mindfulness exercises and one of the meditation exercises for at least five minutes every day over the next week.
2. Each week for the next five weeks, see if you can increase the length of the exercises until you are practicing at least fifteen minutes in the morning and fifteen minutes at night.

As you practice your mindfulness skills, your ability to do the other exercises in this book, such as observing your thoughts and emotions, will increase as well.

Only those who meditate regularly
can judge whether or not it is worthwhile.

- You are the conscious observer of your thoughts and experiences, and you can choose from what perspective you view them at any given time. When you experience a negative emotion about a situation, take a step back, disengage, and gain a new perspective so that you can see what is really going on.

- You are a conscious being continuously in the process of becoming; you are not stuck with a defined identity based on your personal history. When you start feeling limited by your past, just remember that the events of the past are like rocks in a stream, and you are the water constantly flowing forward.

- Without awareness of your thoughts and emotions in the present moment, you have no ability to change. Mindfulness and meditation teach you the skills for being in the present so you can increase your awareness of your internal process and make active choices about it.

- Mindfulness involves being aware of each thought, feeling, and sensation that arises. You can be mindful anywhere and anytime. You simply have to draw your attention to the present moment and observe what is happening.

- Meditation is the practice of focusing your thought process. Through meditation you develop the skill to determine where your attention goes.

- Practice mindfulness and at least one meditation exercise daily, and you will be able to shape your experiences by choosing where you focus your attention and thoughts.

Chapter 7

Knowing What You Value

To live is to choose. But to choose well,
you must know who you are and what you stand for.
—Kofi Annan

You now have more awareness of how your thoughts, beliefs, and actions affect how you create your future. The next step is to learn some concrete skills to help you use your valuable thought and behavioral resources effectively to move you closer to what you want. As you know, wanting is the future-oriented state that can move us toward thriving. Reaching for new things is how we continue to grow and evolve as humans. However, people often get stuck in the thriving process because they have difficulty identifying clearly what they want or why they want it. Or sometimes they get distracted by wanting so many different things that they never really get anywhere. In this chapter you will learn how what you value in life shapes what you want, which will prepare you to set meaningful goals, a topic we'll discuss in the next chapter. When you base your goals on your value system and when they hold real meaning, you are far more likely to stay focused and maintain the motivation to stay the course.

The Value of Feeling Good

We all want to feel good, and we always strive hardest for the things we believe will make us happy. Feeling good, however, is about much more than just the emotion itself. Feeling good indicates that we perceive ourselves to be in the process of improving our experience and growing in some way. Whether we are reaching for a red sports car, a better relationship, or a state of spiritual enlightenment — things we believe will make us feel better if we have them — what we are really reaching for is the state of thriving we believe these things will lead us to. Particularly in Western cultures, people often seek physical items to represent their state of thriving; but the physical things by themselves, whatever they may be, are often of little value. Physical things are only of value when attaining them promotes our survival, causes us to grow, and/or makes us feel how we want to feel. If someone wants a Ferrari, what he really wants is the way the car will make him feel when driving it. The positive feeling may come from believing that driving the car makes him more attractive to others or communicates a high status; or it may simply feel enjoyable to go fast.

If, however, you gave that person the car but put it in a glass box and told him he could never use it, his desire for it would drop dramatically because he wouldn't be able to experience the feeling of excitement, a state of perceived thriving, that would come from driving the car. He would quickly turn his attention to finding something else that led to a desired state of thriving. When people attach too much importance to any physical object or a single wanted destination, they often become fixated on wanting that object, and they may begin to mistakenly believe that *only* that object or destination will lead to the improved state of being. If they are unable to attain it, they can become very frustrated.

While we reach for the good feeling, the things that feel best tend to promote our evolution. Our societies have all evolved because we continue to pursue improvements in our experience. One of the realities of modern life, however, is that we are continually bombarded with messages about what promotes our ability to thrive, providing an often-distorted idea of how to achieve a true state of thriving. While these messages can come from many sources, including our friends and family, they very often come in the form of advertising and media promotion. If you want to sell something to people, the best way to do it is to tell them that not having it will affect their ability to thrive in some way. The message that using a certain product will make you more attractive to the opposite sex is used to sell almost anything, from cars to perfume to chewing gum to nose-hair clippers. Why? Because being attractive to the opposite sex is of high survival, and thriving, value.

These constant messages often cause us to believe that we need lots of things to feel good. If we pursue things simply for the good feeling they may give us, with no sense of how they may cause us to grow or evolve as people, we become trapped in the pursuit of items that are only temporarily fulfilling. Most people have had the experience of feeling good when they go shopping, only to have the feeling fade very quickly once they get home with their purchases. There is nothing inherently wrong with shopping, but if you realize that what you are seeking when you reach for that new dress, fancy stereo, or red Ferrari is a way to promote your ability to thrive, and that thriving is about improving your life experience, you may recognize that there are other ways to do this that will lead to more lasting satisfaction.

Activities such as creating meaningful relationships, engaging in purposeful work, and pursuing your creative passions all lead to feeling good while increasing your ability to thrive. Remember, we all have limited resources, whether these resources are time, money, or energy; you want to put your resources toward activities that have intrinsic value and create greater personal meaning.

WHAT WE VALUE

How you feel about anything is determined by what you value. Even if you choose to do something that feels unpleasant, if you examine the situation closely, you will see that your choice likely stems from your desire to live in accordance with your values. For example, if you watch your best friend perform at an amateur comedy hour, you may do so not because you think the jokes will be good and you will enjoy them — they might be painfully bad — but because being a good friend feels better than being someone who selfishly shirks the duties of friendship. Maintaining good friendships is an activity with very high thrive value.

Values are simply your ideals and your beliefs about what matters to you and what will make your life the best it can be. While everyone has a different set of values, everyone values the things they perceive will promote their ability to thrive. While we assign a value to everything we come in contact with — *I like this better than that* — we tend to think of the things we value as what we hold dearest to us and what gives our life meaning. Our values consist of internal and personal factors, which most people think of as traits or qualities, such as honesty, love, and respect, as well as external, apersonal factors, such as health, fun, and adventure.[1] Values are essentially the things you consider worthwhile. When there is not enough of what you value in your life, you may feel distressed or like the quality of your life is poor. Increasing the presence of these things in your life will greatly promote your well-being.

Your values are not a list of what you have already achieved; rather, they are a list of what you aspire to. They play a large role in how you create your future because they represent your highest priorities and deepest driving forces. Knowing what you value and what matters most to you will help you determine what you want, make the best choices, and point you in the right direction.

Your values are formed by your experiences. They are influenced by your parents and family, your religious affiliation, your friends and peers, your education, the books you read, your society, and more. Whether or not you are aware of them, they impact every aspect of your life, including work, love, play, spirituality, and physical well-being. You demonstrate what you value through all your actions. You use what you value to make decisions and manage your priorities. You build your goals and derive your life purpose from what you value.

A gap between your values and your actions leads to distress. If you value open communication but are having a difficult time talking to your partner, this situation will not feel good to you. Knowing what you value can help you identify sources of distress and begin to evaluate solutions.

As we know, while we have been given the wonderful gift of freedom to think and behave any way that we choose, thought and behavior remain limited resources. How we allocate those resources determines what we achieve, and in order to create the best life possible, we want to spend our resources as wisely as we can. Knowing what you value helps you prioritize the allocation of your resources. When you have a clear sense of what matters most to you, it is easier to know where to direct your energy. Every day there are an infinite number of things you can do and choices you can make. Without knowing what you value, it is easy to get distracted and wander around making decisions that don't lead you anywhere. When you know what is most important to you, your decisions become clearer and easier.

Knowing what to prioritize will help you pinpoint where you want to spend your resources. If open communication is not a top value for feeling good in your relationship, and commitment is instead, you may decide that as long as your partner is loyal, that is what you need to feel satisfied and that it isn't necessary to invest the resources necessary to engage in more open communication. When you make choices and act in ways that are consistent with your values, you will feel a greater sense of internal alignment and well-being.

IDENTIFYING WHAT YOU VALUE

Before you can begin mapping out the path to greater well-being, you need to know where you are starting from. The best way to do this is to examine what you value.

Remember that values are generally not specific things but qualities or idealized states. As you start to identify what you value, if *I value red sports cars* comes to mind, for example, ask yourself why. What is it about red sports cars that you like? How do they make you feel? It is easy to make the mistake of thinking it is a thing we value because of the meaning we have assigned to it. Most things by themselves, though, are meaningless objects, just as money by itself is nothing more than paper with ink on it; we have assigned numeric value to it, which allows us to exchange it for things we want. Knowing what quality you value in something can help open up other possibilities when you can't have that specific thing. For example, if you want to go to Harvard but don't get in, knowing that you want to go there because you value a good education will open up the possibility of considering other schools where you can still receive a quality education. If *things* are what pop into your mind as you begin to create your list of values, keep asking yourself why you value those things until you come up with *qualities* that you connect with these things that you would like to have in your life.

You can hold many values in life, and you will likely have different values for

WORKSHEET: RANK YOUR VALUES

Below is a list of common qualities or states that people value. It is not an exhaustive list, so if you think of others, please write them down on a blank sheet of paper. Review the list, then rank, in order of importance, the top five values in each area of your life. You should choose five values, ranked 1 through 5, for each area. There may be many values you consider important that do not get ranked because they are not in the top five.

Values	Work	Love	Play	Spirituality	Physical Well-Being
Achievement					
Adventure					
Calm/peace					
Challenge					
Collaboration					
Compassion					
Competence					
Competition					
Courage					
Creativity					
Dependability					
Dignity					
Discipline/order					
Excellence					
Fairness					
Flexibility					
Friendliness					
Fun/enjoyment					
Generosity					
Getting along/harmony					
Health					
Helping others					
Honesty					
Independence					
Individuality					
Innovation					
Intellectual stimulation					
Loyalty					
Open communication					
Persistence					
Respect					
Responsibility					
Security					
Wisdom					

Worksheet 7.1   From *Think Forward to Thrive* © 2014 by Jennice Vilhauer, PhD

the various areas of your life, such as work, love, and play. You may value independence at work but not in love. Knowing what you value in the different areas of life will help you choose how to focus your time, thoughts, and energy as you begin to build the life you desire.

Values also tend to have a hierarchy, and knowing clearly what values are most important to us can help us make good choices in our day-to-day life. For example, you may value enjoying delicious food but also value your health. When you are given the choice of eating chocolate cake or a spinach salad, you might remind yourself how much you want to be healthy and to meet your weight-loss goal. When you are clear about which values matter most to you and you are focusing on them regularly, they become more accessible to you, making your decisions much easier. The assignments on the next few pages are designed to help you begin identifying and prioritizing what you value in the various areas of your life. When you get to the next chapter, which is on goal setting, you will have a clearer sense of what is most meaningful to you and what you aspire to, and you will be ready to create the specific goals that will help get you there.

TOP FIVE LIST

Now that you have ranked your values in different areas of your life, it is time to narrow the list to those with the very greatest meaning, which will represent the core values for the designated area of your life. Copy the top-ranked value from each category to the worksheet "My Top Five Life Values," on page 126. If you find it impossible to limit yourself to one in each category, feel free to pick more, but keep in mind that the goal here is to identify the top values that will drive your life. This list is intended to represent where you are right now. What you value can change quite a bit, based on your experiences and what stage of life you are in. When you are twenty you will likely have a different set of values than when you are in your forties, possibly with a family and a mortgage.

Next, define these values so they aren't just words on a page. Create language to capture the spirit of each value — what does it mean to you? For example, if independence is your top value in the area of work, you might define it as *Being able to work on my own without much supervision or interference from others*. Now ask yourself why this value is important to you. Be as specific as you can. This will help you to develop a sense of your worldview. Once you have defined a value and identified why it is important to you, review what you have written, and ask yourself: *What types of actions represent this value?* Write these actions down; these are the things you can do to start living in accordance with your values.

VALUES STATEMENT

Having defined the core values in the various areas of your life, you can now put them together into a values statement that represents how you want to lead your life and behave in the world. Values statements are assertions about how you value yourself, other people, your community, and the world. Values statements describe actions, which are the living enactment of the fundamental values you hold.

To begin writing your values statement, review your top five list and look for themes. You may notice that you carry certain values consistently across all five areas, such as "helping others." Incorporate in your statement the name of each value you're including, the reasons you hold these values, and any actions or feelings that capture the value's meaning to you. It isn't necessary to use everything you wrote in your worksheet, only the things that really resonate with you.

Frame each sentence in the present tense, since these are aspirational statements based on what you value now and what you aspire to. As you encounter new experiences, your values will change; you can always modify the statement later. Remember, the statement does not need to reflect what you are currently doing in your life but rather what you currently value. Here's an example:

My Values Statement

I value the ability to live independently and the freedom to express myself creatively so that I can always produce my best work and live to my full potential. I value choosing activities that bring calm and relaxation into my life so that I rejuvenate and care for myself. I make the effort to openly and fearlessly communicate with others because I value close and strong relationships.

MY VALUES STATEMENT

WORKSHEET: MY TOP FIVE LIFE VALUES

Value	My Definition	Why Do I Value This?	Actions
Example (work): *Independence*	*Being able to work on my own without much supervision or interference from others.*	*I believe I think better and produce my best work when I have adequate freedom to do so.*	*Ask for a work-from-home day once a week. Work for myself.*
Work 1.			
Love 2.			
Play 3.			
Spirituality 4.			
Physical well-being 5.			

Worksheet 7.2

PRACTICE ASSIGNMENTS

1. Complete the "Rank Your Values" worksheet on page 123.
2. Transfer your top value in each of the five categories of work, love, play, spirituality, and physical well-being to the "My Top Five Life Values" worksheet on page 126. Work through each of your top values, following the steps in this chapter, to clearly define what it means to you.
3. Use your top five values to create your "Values Statement" on page 125, which will reflect who you aspire to be in the world.

Tips for Thriving

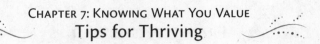

- What we value most is the ability to thrive, which always comes with a good feeling.
- Things themselves have little meaning unless they help us to thrive. Know what qualities you value in the things you desire so that you can open up other possibilities for ways to experience those values.
- Your values determine how you feel about everything. Knowing what you truly value can help guide you in the decisions you make about what you want and the goals you set for yourself.
- Increasing the presence of what you value will promote your sense of well-being.
- Use what you value to inform your choices, deter yourself from distractions, and better allocate your resources.
- Don't limit yourself by believing that only one thing can make you feel a certain way. There are lots of ways to thrive, so be open to possibilities.

Chapter 8

SETTING YOUR GOALS

A goal without a plan is just a wish.
—ANTOINE DE SAINT-EXUPÉRY

You should now have a clear sense of what you stand for, what you want your life to be about, and in what direction you want to head. The next step is to draw a road map to get you there. Goal setting is a powerful tool for intentionally taking charge of your life; goals are the means by which you move toward the future you are creating. In this chapter you will learn basic skills to help you set goals and avoid common mistakes.

THERE IS NO FINAL DESTINATION

As we know well by now, from the FDT perspective, thriving is a continuous state of becoming. The things we want and the goals we set are not final destinations. It is the process, the journey of reaching for something, that promotes our growth. Often people are afraid to make a choice about what they want because they fear making a mistake and ending up stuck somewhere they don't want to be. But keep in mind that every time you complete a goal and arrive somewhere, you will find that your arrival has led to a new perspective that shows you there is somewhere else to go. You will never achieve it all, because there is always something more. You can never get stuck somewhere, because there is always another choice to make. This is the beauty and excitement of life. Each achievement gives you a new vantage point from which to look around and see all the things you never saw before and all the wonderful places you can go. The point is to simply go somewhere. There is no right or wrong place; each different choice will take you on a different journey, and every journey will open up more possibilities and teach you something new.

Thriving is a continuous state of becoming.

BUILDING GOALS BASED ON YOUR VALUES

You can achieve an infinite number of things and set an infinite number of goals for yourself. The key to developing goals that will lead to deeper thriving is to choose goals that are consistent with your value system. As we saw in the previous chapter, your values are the foundation of your ideal life. If you develop goals that build on that foundation, they will take you in the right direction and help you with the many choices you will need to make along the way.

Building goals that are based on your value system gives you focus and will help keep you from getting blocked by obstacles that may come up along the way. When you choose goals in accordance with your values, you will discover that there are many different ways to achieve a goal, and you'll be less likely to give up when one way of doing it doesn't work out. You will be far less likely to sabotage the goals you create if these goals are not attempts to solve unrelated problems or driven by ineffective thought patterns.

When you know what you want to achieve, you know where you should concentrate your efforts and resources; the choices along the way become clearer because you now have direction. For example, if your goal is to do well in school because you value excellence in your personal life and achievement in your career life, and you have the choice to go to a movie with a friend or stay home and study for your exam tomorrow, the choice to see the movie might be tempting, but staying home to study will seem easier because you have a bigger-picture view of what you aspire to.

The first step toward building goals that are consistent with your values is deciding specifically what you want. This is one of the most difficult steps for many people, so if you get stuck, refer back to your values statement on page 125 and concentrate on who you are aspiring to be.

HOW DO YOU DECIDE WHAT YOU WANT?

Knowing what you want is the first and most important step in creating a better future. But how do you make this important decision? For many people this is the first hurdle, and some never get over it. Trying to decide what they want seems overwhelming. If you have already reviewed your values list and still find it difficult to decide what you want, try first taking a look at what you don't want.

Most of us have a good idea of what we don't want in life. We look around and see all the terrible things happening in the world, and we realize that we don't want war, we don't want poverty, we don't want sickness. We look at our own lives and think about the things that don't feel right, such as the boss who nags, the spouse who isn't supportive, the kids who don't listen, or the empty checking account. We think, *I don't want to be poor, I don't want to work at this lousy job where no one appreciates me, I don't want to have to deal with the screaming kids who never listen.*

The good news is that because you have identified what you don't want, knowing what you do want is now within your reach. In chapter 2 we discussed the idea that it is the contrast between two states that allows us to detect the existence of one or the other. If there were no contrasts, we would exist in a state of nothingness. If we know we don't want something, it is because we believe some preferable state exists; otherwise, we wouldn't know that what we were experiencing was unwanted.

While knowing what you don't want gives you a place to start, if you stop there, you will never generate any thoughts or actions to improve the situation, because you have not yet identified what you do want. Once you have identified what you don't want, see if you can flip it over and find the contrasting wanted state. If you don't want to walk somewhere, perhaps that is because you know you would rather be driving; if you don't want to work in a retail job but you aren't sure what kind of job you would like, write down as many details as possible about what you dislike about retail, then see if you can flip over each detail to create a list of what you would like in a job. For example: *I don't like retail because it is exhausting to stand on my feet all day. Instead, I would like a job where I could spend more time at a desk.* Once you have identified something you don't want, look at it and ask yourself:

ASK YOURSELF
What would I like to see instead?

Examples:
Don't want: I don't want a spouse who doesn't appreciate me.
Want: I want a spouse who adores me and treats me with respect.
Don't want: I don't want to work at this lousy job.
Want: I want a job that stimulates me intellectually and allows me to be creative.

Get as specific as possible. Once you have decided you want a job that is stimulating and creative, start thinking about other aspects of the job you would like, such as independence, a lot of interaction with coworkers, increased responsibility, a better salary. The more details you include, the more specific you can be in developing the plan and the steps necessary to achieve your goal.

Deciding what you want today does not mean you can't change your mind tomorrow. Often we think we want something, but as we find out more about it we change our minds. Consider this a success, not a failure! It doesn't mean you don't know what you want. It means you know you want something else instead. Focus on that "something else instead" and go in that direction. Deciding that you don't want something you thought you did just means you are making a more informed decision with new data that wasn't available to you before; it is not the same as giving up when things get difficult. Also, keep in mind that there is no final destination. As mentioned earlier, every time you obtain something you want, you have a new perspective from which to see other possibilities. Choosing something you want doesn't mean you give up all the other possibilities; it means you open the door to possibilities you didn't know existed.

Use the "Identifying What You Want" worksheet on the next page (p. 133) to write down all the things you don't want, then use these things to inform the other side of the list, which asks you to identify what you do want. Once you have your list, review it to see which items are consistent with your values statement. Place a star next to those items, because those will be a good place to start.

Scott was an attorney who hated his job. He had been doing the same thing for fifteen years and felt stuck. When he was asked what else he would like to do, his usual response was a blank stare; then he would say, "I don't know — I guess that's why I am stuck." So Scott was asked to write out a list of everything he didn't like about his job. He already had spent so much time focused on this that he found it a very easy task. *I hate my boss for always nagging me and micromanaging everything I do, I hate my coworkers who gossip and backstab, I hate the lack of creativity, I hate the long hours.* The list ended up being quite long. Once Scott was done, we took a look at his list, and for each item he had written down he then found the flip side. He came up with the following: *I want a boss who trusts my work and allows me to be more independent, I want to work with people who are caring and trustworthy, I want to experience more creativity at work, I want to work reasonable hours so I can still enjoy the rest of my life.* When Scott read over the list of things he wanted, he was quite surprised. "I never thought I could have a job like that, so I've never dared to even dream about it." While Scott didn't yet have the job he wanted, he had taken the first and most important step, which was to identify in what direction he wanted to head.

WORKSHEET: IDENTIFYING WHAT YOU WANT

Things I Don't Like in My Life	What Would I Like Instead?
Example: *I hate the apartment I live in because it is so noisy.*	**Example:** *I would prefer to live in an environment that is more soothing so that I can feel at peace when I am there.*
1.	1.
2.	2.
3.	3.
4.	4.
5.	5.
6.	6.
7.	7.
8.	8.
9.	9.
10.	10.

Worksheet 8.1

From *Think Forward to Thrive* © 2014 by Jennice Vilhauer, PhD

The Presence of What You Want

As you think about what you do want instead of what you don't, write down what you want in the *presence of* state discussed in chapter 4. For example, if you recognize that you don't want an abusive partner and you decide that you want a partner who doesn't abuse you, you still haven't identified the presence of what you do want. All you have identified is the absence of abuse. Listing the presence of what you want achieves several crucial things. To start with, as we've discussed, it activates the thought, which then allows for other similar thoughts to grow around it. As the thoughts around what you want grow, the brain's problem-solving system, which will help you achieve what you want, becomes active. Most important, identifying what you want in the *presence of* state allows you to visualize what you want, an essential tool for reaching a goal. This is because the brain only has the ability to picture doing something. You cannot visualize *not* doing something without picturing yourself doing something else.

Example:
Picture yourself eating an apple.
Now picture yourself NOT eating the apple.
What are you DOING?
- *Looking* at the apple.
- *Standing* next to the apple.
- *Holding* the apple.

Notice all the verbs? In order for the brain to conjure up a visual image of your doing anything, there must be the presence of some type of action. In other words, you need to take into account your brain's need for the presence of action when creating your goals.

Example:
- *I want to quit smoking.* This goal by itself doesn't give you anything else to visualize. The only image it conjures up is smoking.
- *I want to lead a healthy life.* This is a better goal, with good visualization potential. You can begin to visualize what leading a healthy life might look like and what types of healthy activities you could be engaged in. Smoking is not one of them.

While you will learn much more about visualization in chapter 9, for now work on creating goals that you can visualize by identifying the presence of something you want. Once you know what you want and can conjure up a picture of it in your head, you are on your way to a powerful and achievable goal.

WHY DO YOU WANT IT?

Once you have identified something you want, ask yourself:

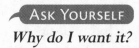

ASK YOURSELF
Why do I want it?

We often want something because we believe it will solve an unrelated problem. This commonly occurs when we set goals that involve changing our external circumstances, believing that this will change how we feel on the inside. For example, I want a relationship so I can finally be happy, or I want a better job so I can stop feeling like a loser. As you well know by now, contrary to what many people think, the way we feel inside is not controlled by our external environment but rather by what we believe about the external environment. Often we try to solve unrelated problems with the goals we set because we're caught in ineffective patterns of thinking. When you ask yourself why you want what you want, you are forced to take a closer look at the actual problem you are trying to solve.

Examples:

Goal: I want to lose weight.
Why: I'm afraid if I don't, no one will ever love me.
Real problem: I believe I am unlovable, and I really want someone to love me.
Better goal: I want to work on feeling lovable.

Goal: I want to lose weight.
Why: My doctor said I am at risk for a heart attack and I feel anxious about it.
Real problem: My weight is putting my health at risk and it is preventing me from achieving what I really want, which is to be healthier and lead a more active life.
Better goal: I want to work on being healthier and leading an active life, which includes achieving a healthy weight.

Goal: I want a red sports car.
Why: So people will like me more and pay more attention to me.
Real problem: I feel people don't like me the way I am.
Better goal: I want to work on liking myself and not worrying about what others think.

When you set a goal for the purpose of solving an unrelated problem, you will have very little motivation to work on the goal because achieving it won't help you get what you really want. This is one reason why it's so important to spend the time defining what you want.

Often, when you set a goal to solve an unrelated problem, you're trying to escape some type of fear. For example, *I am afraid of being a failure so I'd better be a high achiever at work*. Fear-based statements imply you are worried that if you don't accomplish your goal, something bad will happen: *I have to do this or else, I know I should do this, If I don't do this someone will be angry with me, If I don't accomplish this I am a loser*. When you approach a goal out of fear, you expend valuable resources by thinking about something you don't want in an effort to get something you do want. While you might get some impetus out of scaring yourself into action, people who do this tend to lose their motivation more quickly and don't get as much satisfaction out of their achievements. Ideally, you want to set goals from a position of hope so that when you think about achieving them you feel enthusiasm, excitement, and eagerness. When you feel these kinds of positive emotions, you know that you are focused on what you want and that you are maximizing your thought resources.

WHAT IF YOU CAN'T HAVE WHAT YOU WANT?

Sometimes when people begin this process they bump up against what seem like very real obstacles, which prevents them from realizing their goals and dreams. One client, Oscar, had been in an accident several years ago in which his car had caught fire and left him with burn marks on one side of his face. Oscar stated that what he wanted most was to be completely healed and no longer have the disfiguring scarring on his face. When asked what bothered him most about his scars, he stated that he felt they prevented him from feeling confident and socializing with others because he feared he would be rejected. He stated that he wanted to be healed of his scars so he could enjoy more social interactions, and in particular he wanted to be able to date and eventually get married. Oscar was deeply depressed because he believed the disfiguring scars would prevent him from ever having the things he wanted. He had become increasingly isolated since his accident and rarely left his home. Once Oscar could identify *why* he wanted to be healed of his scars, it was easy for him to see that it was what he *anticipated* the scars would prevent him from doing that was causing his distress. Oscar was indeed struggling with a very real and very unwanted situation. He would probably never be healed of all the scarring on his face. What was preventing Oscar from having what he wanted was not this very real situation, but rather his expectations about how others would perceive him and how this would limit his life. Expectations, as you well know by now, are about things that have not happened, but they drive our responses because we believe they *will* happen.

We all have to deal with things we don't desire. Illness, a job loss, a car accident, the death of a loved one — the reason we don't want these things is that we believe they prevent us from being able to have something we want and inhibit our thriving. If you've been doing your reading, you know that it is what we expect these things will mean for our future that causes our unhappiness.

But can the unwanted things in life *prevent* you from having what you do want in your future? Sometimes, but probably much less than you realize. If you had always dreamed of having dinner at the Windows on the World restaurant at the very top of the World Trade Center in Manhattan, this is a specific experience you won't be able to have because the very unwanted and very real terrorist attack on September 11, 2001, destroyed the WTC towers. Something that was possible no longer is, but again, asking yourself *why* you wanted it can help you come up with an alternative experience that might still allow you to achieve a similar state of thriving. Perhaps there is another fine restaurant with beautiful views of Manhattan that you could enjoy.

When you bump up against a situation in which you feel you can't have what you want, remember to ask yourself *why* you want it, since doing so may give you the clarity to see whether your belief is based on real facts or expectations about future events. If you discover it is an expectation, then go back to chapter 4 and work through the steps on how to create a *new* expectation.

DEVELOPING THE GOAL

Once you have identified what you want and the reason you want it, you are ready to set specific goals that will help you attain those things. The process of goal setting has been well studied, and many established techniques are used by successful people in all fields. One of the first things to do is to distinguish between a long-term and a short-term goal. A long-term goal should be the big-picture objective that brings you closer to living in accordance with your values. For example, if your personal value is to live in financial freedom, then a long-term goal might be to pay off all your debt. While there is no definitive time frame for distinguishing long-term goals from short-term ones, anything that will take longer than a year to achieve would safely fit into the long-term category. Once you have defined your long-term goal, you then break it down into smaller and smaller steps that you must take.

Example:
  Long-term goal: I would like to make a career change and become a writer.
  Short-term goals:
    ◻ I need to write my first book.
      ◻ I need to write the first chapter.
        ◻ I need to write an outline.
          ◻ I need to write the first page.

One widely used mnemonic that helps people design specific steps to building good, actionable goals is SMART. The acronym stands for:

S Specific: The goal should be clear and well-defined so you can map the steps.

M Measurable: There must be a way to tell when you have achieved the goal.

A Attainable: You must believe the goal is attainable.

R Relevant: The goal should be consistent with your values and lead you closer to who you aspire to be.

T Time-bound: You should set deadlines to motivate yourself.

Let's look at these one at a time.

SPECIFIC

The goals you intend to work toward should be as specific as possible. When you set a vague goal, it is hard to define the steps that will get you there. If you state that your goal is to feel better, what does that really mean or look like to you? How would you know you were feeling better? Who else would notice? What would you do differently if you were feeling better? If you know you will be feeling better when you start going to the gym three days a week or when you start a new dance class, use those as your specific goals instead of something vague like feeling better. When your goal is specific, you will be able to clearly define the steps and take actions toward getting there.

People often set goals that sound good but have no real actionable steps. For example, *I want to go on a vacation.* Most people would think this is a nice goal. But the reality is that it is not specific enough to allow you to take any real steps. Where do you want to go? *I want to go to Europe.* Okay, that is an improvement, but still too vague. There are no plane tickets to Europe. You will have to pick a specific country and then a city within a country before you can take an actionable step toward getting there, for example: *I want to buy a plane ticket to Madrid, Spain.*

Many people, when they are setting goals, get stuck at the *I want to go to Europe* stage. As you are setting your goals, ask yourself:

ASK YOURSELF
Can I identify an actionable step I can take?

MEASURABLE

When you achieve a goal, it leads to increased satisfaction and greater self-esteem. However, if your goal isn't measurable, it will be hard to know when you have reached it. For example, if your goal is to lead a more joyful life, you need to define how you will know when you have reached that point. For example, *I will know I am leading a more joyful life when I wake up excited to get out of bed five days a week.*

Sometimes it is useful to measure progress toward a goal before you have made it all the way there. This lets you know how close you are to achieving the goal so that, if necessary, you can make adjustments along the way. In order to measure the progress of a goal you need to know where you are starting from, so your goal should also include a baseline measurement: *I will know I am leading a more joyful life when I go from never wanting to get out of bed to waking up excited to get out of bed five days a week.*

ATTAINABLE

Do you believe you can achieve your goal? You will take the actions necessary to achieve your goal only if you believe it is possible. People can believe things on two levels — the intellectual level and the feeling level. The intellectual level usually relates to your conscious thoughts. The feeling level reflects not only your conscious thoughts but also your stored unconscious beliefs. If you think one thing but feel another, then your belief about the situation is probably not deep enough for you to take action on it.

In other words, people act on sincere belief. Answer this question: Do you believe it is possible to get a job making six dollars an hour? This is below minimum wage in most states, and the majority of people would probably say *yes.* Now answer this question: Do you think you can get a job making one million dollars a year? Since less than 1 percent of people in the United States earn this kind of income, the majority of people would probably say *no.*

When most people are asked why they don't think they could make a million dollars a year, they generally offer answers such as:

- *I don't have enough education.*
- *I don't have enough experience.*
- *I don't have the right skills for those types of jobs.*

People act on sincere belief.

There are, however, many examples to prove that none of these reasons needs to prevent you from making a million dollars a year.

- *I don't have enough education.* Many people without college degrees earn more than a million dollars a year. Bill Gates and the developers of Facebook are college dropouts worth well over a billion dollars.
- *I don't have enough experience.* There are teenagers who are earning more than a million dollars a year, such as Fraser Doherty, who at age fourteen started making jam from his grandmother's recipes and selling it on the internet.
- *I don't have the right skills for those types of jobs.* There are many stories of people who start companies and make millions without any experience in the field or with very little skill, such as the man who launched a company that cleans dog poop out of people's backyards, then sold franchises worth more than three million dollars.

Do you feel compelled to put down this book and go out and look for a job making a million dollars a year?

Probably not, because despite being presented with facts that are inconsistent with what you consciously believe, you still don't *feel* as if you could find a job making that much money. On an unconscious level you probably still hold beliefs that you wouldn't really be able to do it. Therefore, the likelihood that you will take actions that would lead to a job earning a million dollars a year is very low.

The degree of your belief in something will correlate to the amount of effort you put forth — if you believe something has only a 50 percent chance of happening, you will likely give only 50 percent effort. As we've learned, this relationship between belief and effort leads to self-fulfilling prophecies. The more you believe something is possible, the more effort you will put toward making it happen, so the more likely it is to actually happen. The less you believe something is possible, the less effort you will put forth to make it happen, which makes it less likely that it will happen.

While the goals you set need to feel doable, they should also feel challenging enough that you will know you have grown once you have achieved them. As we know, as human beings we seek growth, since this is part of what allows us to keep reaching for new states of thriving. When we set goals that are too easy or that don't challenge us, we don't feel much motivation to achieve them. If your goal is to get your life organized, and you set the goal of cleaning out your wallet, that probably won't excite you nearly as much as if you set the goal of meeting with a professional organizer to evaluate how to organize your entire house. Why? Because imagining a clean wallet doesn't feel nearly as good as imagining a completely clutter-free home. It is important to strike a balance: choose goals that feel challenging but that are within the realm of possibility. If you are feeling really stuck, remember that it is better to start small than not to start at all.

Chrystal had the goal of getting married and having kids, but she refused to date. She said it made her too uncomfortable to think of going through the process of trying to get to know strangers and playing all the dating games. In fact, whenever she thought about it she felt overwhelmed by fear. She had been rejected by several men in the past for reasons she didn't understand, and she was worried it could happen again. Because of this, setting the goal of going out on a date was too big for her. Instead, Chrystal set a goal for herself that felt much more doable, which was to learn as much as she could about dating and relationship behavior. She signed up for several courses on the subject given by experts in the dating field, and she created a list of books that she could read that would teach her more about the dating process. Chrystal felt that if she could understand men and relationships better, she would have less to fear and would be more willing to take that next step later.

RELEVANT

The choices you can make are infinite. You can set goals and strive toward many things, so how do you prevent yourself from becoming scattered and unfocused, setting inconsistent goals, and/or unnecessarily wasting time? The best way to avoid these pitfalls is to set goals that reflect your values statement (page 125), which should be the foundation for the things you choose to achieve in life. Remembering that the values statement is meant to be aspirational, review the statement and look for gaps between your present behavior and the value system you aspire to live by. Any goals that help you close this gap or live in a way that is consistent with your values statement will be relevant in moving you toward a more satisfying future.

TIME-BOUND

Setting a concrete time frame for achieving your goals is an essential motivational factor. The time frame needs to push you but still allow enough time to achieve the goal. If you tell yourself you need to lose five pounds in ten years, how hard will you work at it every day? On the other hand, if you tell yourself you need to lose five pounds by tomorrow, you probably won't even try.

Having a time frame creates an internal sense of urgency that pushes you to take action and leads to more rapid achievement. Additionally, setting a time limit within which you plan to achieve your goal helps you plan the time frame for necessary short-term accomplishments along the way. For example, if you plan to write a twelve-chapter book in one year, you know that you need to plan to complete at least a chapter a month in order to stay on target. If each chapter has approximately thirty pages, then you know that you must write at least one page a day.

You are now ready to begin the process of creating truly SMART goals. Use the worksheets at the end of the chapter to guide you through the process.

The more you believe something is possible,
the more effort you will put toward making it happen.

PRACTICE ASSIGNMENTS

1. Complete the "Achieving My Goal" worksheet on page 144. Ask yourself all the questions so that you will be well prepared to establish SMART goals on the next worksheet.

2. Complete the "Creating Goals" worksheet on page 145. Start with the big picture of where you want to go, and then establish short-term SMART goals to begin mapping out how you will get there. There is no goal too small, as long as it is a step in the right direction.

WORKSHEET: ACHIEVING MY GOAL

My goal — what I want:

_____

Why do I want this? Am I trying to solve an unrelated problem? Is this goal coming from a place of fear or true desire?

_____

What value is this goal consistent with?

_____

Are any doubts coming into my mind about my ability to achieve this goal?

_____

How will I feel when I achieve this goal?

_____

What are the specific steps I must take?

_____

What can I do today that will bring me closer to my goal?

_____

What can I do tomorrow that will bring me closer to my goal?

_____

What can I do every day this week that will bring me closer to my goal?

_____

Worksheet 8.2   From *Think Forward to Thrive* © 2014 by Jennice Vilhauer, PhD

WORKSHEET: CREATING GOALS

Big-Picture Value: (Example: *Financial independence*)

Long-Term Goal: (Example: *Pay off debt*)

Short-Term Goal:
(Example: *Consolidate my bills*)

Short-Term Goal:
(Example: *Call a credit counselor*)

Short-Term Goal:

1.

2.

3.

Goal Checklist

__ Can I identify **S**pecific steps?
__ Is it **M**easurable?
__ Do I believe I can **A**chieve this goal?

No 1 2 3 4 5 6 7 8 9 10 Yes!

__ Is it **R**elevant to my values?
__ Is there a **T**ime frame for achieving this goal?

__ Can I identify **S**pecific steps?
__ Is it **M**easurable?
__ Do I believe I can **A**chieve this goal?

No 1 2 3 4 5 6 7 8 9 10 Yes!

__ Is it **R**elevant to my values?
__ Is there a **T**ime frame for achieving this goal?

__ Can I identify **S**pecific steps?
__ Is it **M**easurable?
__ Do I believe I can **A**chieve this goal?

No 1 2 3 4 5 6 7 8 9 10 Yes!

__ Is it **R**elevant to my values?
__ Is there a **T**ime frame for achieving this goal?

Worksheet 8.3

From *Think Forward to Thrive* © 2014 by Jennice Vilhauer, PhD

Tips for Thriving

- Goal setting is a powerful tool for intentionally taking charge of your life and creating your future.

- Thriving is a continuous state of becoming. The things we want and the goals we set are not final destinations. Each time you achieve something, it gives you a new vantage point from which to see all the wonderful places you can go. The point is to simply go somewhere. There is no right or wrong place; each choice will take you on a different journey, and every journey will teach you something new.

- Knowing what you don't want in life will help you decide what you do want.

- Make sure to identify the *presence of* what you want. Do not state that you want the *absence of* something, like not getting angry with your children. The *presence of* state, such as wanting to be patient with your children, activates the brain's problem-solving ability.

- Once you know what you want, always ask yourself: Why do I want it? Knowing why will keep you from setting a goal in order to solve an unrelated problem, such as trying to lose weight to make your partner love you more.

- Once you know exactly what you want, use the SMART criteria to develop a clearly actionable goal:
    - **S**pecific: The goal should be clear and well-defined so you can map the steps.
    - **M**easurable: There must be a way to tell when you have achieved the goal.
    - **A**ttainable: You must believe the goal is attainable.
    - **R**elevant: The goal should lead you closer to who you aspire to be.
    - **T**ime-bound: You should set a realistic time frame to help motivate yourself.

Chapter 9

VISUALIZING YOUR FUTURE

A picture is worth a thousand words.
—Unknown

If you take a look around, you will see nothing human-made that did not first exist as an image in someone's mind. It is impossible to create something that cannot first be imagined. This is true of your future as well. Visualization helps you use the power of your mind to grow your thoughts around your goals and increase your ability to achieve them.

Psychologists have used visual imagery for years, as a way to help people enhance performance at skill-based activities and create desired emotional states. People who want to learn to shoot basketball hoops can show considerable improvement just by visualizing shooting baskets in their heads. Simply visualizing playing the piano can actually improve someone's ability to play a piece. In other words, being able to do something in your head greatly increases your chances of being able to do it in real life.[1]

The power of visualization is in part due to the way the brain functions. Our awareness about our thought process is largely limited to what we can think about with language, yet only a small part of what we think about happens in a language-based way. In fact, language-based thinking is extremely slow compared with the brain's sensory-based thinking, which occurs at a rate thousands of times faster. And while our language-based thoughts are extremely powerful, and something we want to attend to at all times, it is critical to realize that most of our mental process and information storage occurs in sensory images.[2]

This is why we often respond to visual images much more quickly than we're even conscious of. For example, if you are driving and you see someone in front of you suddenly slam on the brakes, your response — to slam on your own brakes — is a result of your assessment of danger and your move to protect yourself, and it happens almost instantaneously. You don't have time to actually think the words — *I see brake lights; that could be dangerous. I'd better step on my own brakes and slow down.*

Our brains communicate with sensory images not only more rapidly than they do with language but also at deeper levels of consciousness, because most unconscious material is stored this way. Evidence shows that the unconscious part of the mind leads us to take action before we ever have any awareness of our language-based thoughts.[3] That means the sensory-based information stored there is a large driving force behind everything we do.

FUTURE PROJECTIONS

As we know, what we produce in our minds can only come from what is stored there. We anticipate the future based on what we have stored of our past experiences. Much of what we store from the past is in the form of sensory images, and we are constantly projecting future experiences from those stored images. For example, say you play tennis and it's your turn to serve. You get nervous and think about the last time you missed a serve. Your unconscious mind gets the picture and sends a message to the brain's motor center to repeat the same serve, so you miss again. If you want to correct your serve, you have to see yourself serving correctly. This is what top athletes do when they train — they visualize themselves doing it the way they want to do it. Your brain is constantly pulling images from your mind to create future projections. What if you would like to start seeing more success in your future, such as in the areas of relationships or work, but all the stored pictures you have in these areas depict past failures? You must begin to create a new set of projected future images and implant them in your brain so they become part of your stored sensory unconscious.

THE BRAIN IS A PROBLEM-SOLVING MACHINE

The brain is your creative servant. It is there to help you create your future experiences. The brain is an anticipatory mechanism wired to expect that what you anticipate will come true, and it is therefore invested in helping you prepare for the arrival of what you expect. It will help you generate thoughts and solutions you would never have believed you could come up with had you not first set forth the expectation. This is part of the thought-growing process discussed in chapter 2. If you expect to find a great job, then your brain will start to generate ideas about how to make that happen. If you don't expect it, your brain will not do this work. It is not as simple as saying you *want* a better job; you have to literally *expect* and believe that you will find a better job in order for the brain to come up with a way to make that happen. Many people go through life wanting lots of things but never believing they can really have them, so their minds never work on finding ways to bring those things about. As a result, what they want never shows up. This dynamic relates to the idea that we only act on what we believe to be true. Your brain would not work on helping you come up with solutions to things you didn't really expect. That would be a huge waste of its resources.

Changing what we anticipate starts with what we think. However, as we just discussed, our language-based thinking makes up only a small part of the mind's processing ability. To really harness the power of your mind to change expectation, you need to use sensory-based images as well in order to activate deeper, faster, and more automatic levels of processing. Your first visualization of something is like a light switch in your brain — when it is turned on, it triggers the brain to generate a solution or the way to obtain what you are expecting. Many people are so limited by their beliefs about what is possible that they never even flip the switch. This is why it is so vital to think about the presence of what you want as opposed to the absence of what you don't. When you think of the presence of what you want, your brain automatically starts to create that first visual image that flips the switch and turns on your mind's solution-generating process.

As you begin to shift your expectations and to actively direct your thoughts toward what you want, things that you never noticed before in your environment will show up and start to assist you in achieving your goal. This is a result of our limited attentional capacity. As we know, there is far more happening in our environment than we could ever possibly pay attention to all at once.[4] When you start to focus on something specifically, the brain selectively shifts its attention to finding the things in the environment that match up with what you are thinking about. Remember our example from chapter 2 — if you have ever purchased a new car, you may have noticed that suddenly you see the same car everywhere. When you activate an image in your mind and hold your attention on it for a little while, you prime your brain to selectively notice those things that match up. This is why people with depression often notice more negative things in their environment and happier people notice more things to feel happy about. The pattern then feeds itself. If you see depressing things, you will feel more depressed, and then you will look for more depressing things.

While we all live with the illusion that we are aware of what is happening around us, the reality is that our limited attentional capacity allows us only to see a small amount of what is around is. Few people realize that they are active participants in creating what they see in their world and thus what they experience. You can prime your brain using visualization to start attending to things that will help you feel better and help you achieve more of your goals.[5]

Carol wanted to buy her own home, but she had no idea how to go about it. She had grown up in a family in which money was quite limited, and her family had always rented. She loved to visualize herself living in her own place; sometimes on the weekends she would go to home-goods stores such as Pottery Barn just to walk around and see what types of things she would furnish her home with. As she did this, she started to see in her mind even more clearly the house she wanted, and the desire for her own home grew more intense. She felt motivated to start looking at real estate websites and to search the available properties in her area. The more she looked, the more her new home was on her mind during the day. She started to notice signs for real estate agents and properties for sale everywhere she went. One day when Carol was on the internet — though she rarely paid attention to the advertising on websites — an image of a home caught her eye, and as she glanced over at the bottom of her screen she noticed it was an ad offering an information class for first-time home buyers. She called and signed up for the class.

VISUALIZATION

The brain's visualization process works by creating mental pictures based on the mechanics of the visual system. When light reflects off objects in the environment, it is converted into electrical signals that are transmitted through chemicals called neurotransmitters. Your brain then uses these messages to create a mental picture of what you have seen. It does this by interpreting the electrical and chemical impulses. When you use your imagination to visualize something, your brain creates *that* picture using the same method of interpreting electrical and chemical impulses. This is why it is often said that the brain can't tell the difference between what you see and what you imagine. When you use your imagination or mental imagery to project the future, the effect can be just as real as when you see things with your eyes.

This has been demonstrated through the use of brain scan technology, which shows that just imagining something brings about actual physical changes in your brain.[6] When you focus on a projected future image using visualization, you are actually changing your brain structure by forging new neural connections and pathways. The more you focus on the image, the stronger the neural connections you form, and the more real what you are visualizing will start to seem.

You can begin to generate future projections that are more consistent with what you want in life by visualizing the outcomes as you want them to be. As you play these visualizations over and over in your mind, they will seem more believable, which increases the likelihood that you will take congruent actions. One way to make this process even more effective is to increase the detail in your imagery. The things we see around us possess a great deal of detail that we may not even be attending to; however, our brain takes it in, and it gets stored as sensory-image data. If we want our future visualizations to be as vivid as what we see in our environment, then we need to imagine them in such detail that they seem just as real.

PICTURE AND DESCRIBE

The act of creating more details around an image of something you want forces you to generate more mental activity, which increases drive or motivation to obtain it. For example, if you think about wanting a piece of chocolate cake but then immediately dismiss the thought, you may quickly forget about it. However, if you think about a piece of chocolate cake, close your eyes and spend a few minutes really imagining the details, the creamy frosting, the warm, moist cake, how great it would taste, savoring the image until your mouth starts to water, your drive to get a piece of cake will increase dramatically. At this point your brain's natural problem-solving process will go to work helping you develop a plan for how to obtain what you want. You might start to think about stopping at your favorite bakery on the way home from work.

The best way to create detail and grow more thoughts around your simulation is to picture and describe it using all your senses. The goal is to experience what you are visualizing as if you are actually living the experience.

APPLE EXERCISE

You may wish to have someone read this exercise to you out loud while you close your eyes and immerse yourself in the sensory imagery.

Picture an apple. What color is the apple? How big is the apple? Does the apple have any markings on it? Does it have a stem and leaves? Is the apple shiny or dull? Pick up the apple and touch it with both hands. What does the apple feel like? Put the apple to your nose. What does it smell like? Take a bite of the apple. Can you hear the crunch? Can you hear yourself chewing? Can you feel the apple in your mouth? What does the apple taste like? Can you feel yourself swallowing the bite of apple?

You want to be able to experience the full sensation of eating an apple as if you were actually doing it. If you couldn't actually taste the apple, try the exercise again until you can.

All the sensory details are what make the simulation come to life and seem real. Some people struggle initially with visualizing an image in their heads. Start small, focus on whatever image comes to mind, even if it is fuzzy, and work on adding in one detail at a time. When using visualization to achieve a goal, you will want to re-create your simulation regularly to anchor it in your awareness, so if you are working with a complex goal, it's a good idea to write down a list of all the details to help yourself recall each one. However, you must actually visualize the details. Simply writing them down and reading the list primarily activates the language-based side of your thinking; it isn't sufficient to generate the sensory representation you are trying to achieve.

EMOTIONAL INTENSITY

Emotion is another kind of sensory-based representation. Because we know that emotion is preceded by thought, when you feel something deeply, you have achieved enough belief in the subject to make taking action more likely. The goal is to make your visual simulation seem so real that you can actually feel yourself experiencing it. Remember, feelings are the indicator. If you don't feel the experience of the simulation, you have more work to do. When you begin to feel it, you have crossed the threshold leading to action.

EXPOSURE

Since what we produce in our minds can only come from what is stored there, it can be quite difficult to imagine something that has not already happened to us. It would be difficult to create a visual simulation of living on Mars, even if that were something you really wanted to do, because you don't have any experiences of what that would be like. Sometimes, in order to create more detail in a visual simulation, you have to expose yourself to more details in the outside world. For example, if you dream of doing something you've never tried before, such as scuba diving, you may have a difficult time simulating a detailed experience, since you don't have much to draw on. You will need to expose yourself to the experience of scuba diving in order to make the possibility of it seem more real. You may need to read books or watch videos on scuba diving, or ask questions of people you know who have tried it; if you live near the ocean, you may be able to go visit a scuba-diving school. Each of these experiences will give you more data with which to create detail for your mental simulation. Exposing yourself to what you want helps you formulate the steps to making something happen, and it creates opportunity for thoughts to grow around your experiences.

When actual experiences are unavailable, people often use pictures as a way to enhance mental simulations. Someone who wants to lose weight may place a photograph of a slimmer person on the refrigerator. It can be quite useful to begin your simulation this way, by finding pictures that represent what you are trying to achieve and then focusing on the pictures until you can reproduce the images in your mind. Since it is vital to include as many of your senses as possible in the simulation, pictures alone will often not be enough — but they are a great place to start. As you look at the picture, see if you can actually generate the emotion that goes with its content. If you see someone smiling in the picture, see if you can feel the same degree of happiness that the person's smile indicates. For many people, playing the right music can set a mood that matches the emotion they are trying to achieve. For example, if you want to run a marathon, try looking at a picture of a runner while you play the theme from *Chariots of Fire*, then close your eyes and imagine yourself as the runner. As you begin to feel and believe that running the marathon is possible, it becomes more likely that you will put on your running shoes and head out the door for a practice sprint.

CREATING SIMULATIONS OF THE FUTURE

Our brain is constantly simulating experiences as a way to prepare for the future. However, this process happens so naturally that we generally aren't even aware of it, just as we usually aren't aware that we're breathing. If we aren't aware of it, then we are not actively directing the process, and the brain is simply going on autopilot, often re-creating past unwanted experiences. You can begin to actively direct your future simulations by using the following techniques.

You can do two kinds of simulations — outcome and process. An outcome simulation is a sensory-based representation of the final outcome you expect, and a process simulation involves simulating the steps that get you to the final outcome. Research shows that to get the most benefit from simulations, it is best to use both types together. You should always start with an outcome simulation, since this is what drives the motivation for generating process simulations. For example, if you would like to own a new house, and you create a visual image of your new home and then incorporate other senses to evoke what it would feel like to live there, you will start to get excited about the possibility of this experience. However, to really increase the likelihood of your buying your dream home, you will also want to see yourself accomplishing all the necessary steps along the way, such as contacting a realtor, going to open houses, and so on. When you are able to visualize yourself doing something successfully, you are far more likely to create the real experience.

The perspective you take when creating a simulation is quite important. You can create a simulation from the perspective of either an observer or a participant. When you take the perspective of the observer, you see yourself achieving a goal as if you were watching a movie and seeing the future simulation you are creating on the screen. When you create a simulation from the participant perspective, you see the events happening as if you were really taking part in them — you see them happening to you through your own eyes. The research on visualization indicates that taking the perspective of the participant can be a more engaging and powerful method, leading to better outcomes.[7]

OUTCOME SIMULATIONS

1. Visual simulations are most effective when paired with language-based thinking, so the first step is to make a statement about what you want as if you already have it. For example, *I have a fantastic job that brings me personal satisfaction.*
2. The second step is to form a strong visual image in your mind of what this statement looks like.
3. The third step is to add as much detail to the mental picture and incorporate as many physical senses into your image as possible.
4. Once you have created a detailed sensory-based simulation of the experience you desire and you can feel what it will be like when you have achieved the outcome, you are ready to start imagining yourself accomplishing the steps to get there.

PROCESS SIMULATIONS

1. Begin with the outcome you've just visualized, the goal you are trying to achieve.
2. Remember that there are steps to achieving any goal. Once you know what you want the outcome to be, you need to create visual images of yourself taking the necessary actions to turn the outcome simulation into a real experience.
3. You can work forward or backward. It is intuitive for most people to start from where they are and visualize steps toward where they want to go. Working backward from an outcome simulation, however, while a bit more difficult, has some added benefits. Often, when you work forward, you encounter perceived barriers along the way and stop the process before ever getting to your destination. Working backward allows you to visualize steps you may never get to when you work forward.

If you want a new car, start with the outcome — imagine driving the new car. Then imagine what would have happened just before you got the car — imagine yourself at the car dealer signing the papers, then imagine what would have happened just before you signed. Maybe you were walking around the lot looking at cars or test-driving the one you wanted to buy. Moving backward, imagine yourself driving to the lot in your old car. By doing it this way, you make the process start to seem more real before you can get stuck on early obstacles such as not having enough money. With all the mental energy you are investing, you will be more willing to tackle the money obstacle than you would have if you had started with *I want a new car but I don't have enough money.*

Now that you understand the process of visualization, you will be able to use it to help you visualize not only what you want but also how to go about achieving each step along the way. Have fun!

PRACTICE ASSIGNMENTS

1. Find pictures in magazines that symbolize your goal, and paste them on a large poster board. Then add written statements phrased in the present tense about your goal as if you had already achieved it, such as *I am someone who exercises regularly.* To make this assignment even more powerful, take a snapshot of the poster board and make it your computer's desktop or smartphone screen image so that you see it all day long.

2. Set aside time every day to practice visualizing both outcome and process simulations of achieving your goal. Repetition is essential. When you do this regularly, you strengthen your neural networks, which makes the goal seem more real and therefore something you are more likely to take steps toward achieving.

Tips for Thriving

- Visualization is a key tool for building your ability to imagine your desired future. Being able to picture something in your head greatly increases the likelihood of being able to do it in real life.

- The brain is an anticipatory mechanism wired to believe that what you anticipate will come true. Visualization is a rapid way to begin altering your expectations as you plant new visions of success in your mind.

- Your brain uses visual simulations to prepare for what you expect. You can harness the power of visual simulations by creating simulations of what you *want*.

- When creating a simulation, use as much detail and as many of your senses as possible. This helps to activate mental energy and neural activity. A useful way to add detail to any simulation is to *picture and describe*.

- When you haven't been exposed to something you want, it can be hard to imagine enough details to create vivid simulations of it. Exposing yourself to relevant experiences in the real world can help you get the information you need to enhance your simulations.

- To get the best results from an outcome or process simulation, use the participant perspective and see if you can generate the emotional experience you would have in living it. You can enhance emotional experiences with external props such as music and scents.

Chapter 10

GENERATING SOLUTIONS
FOR SUCCESS

When you believe something can be done...
your mind will find the ways to do it.
—DAVID JOSEPH SCHWARTZ

You've got a great goal. You know what you want, and you can see it clearly in your mind's eye. Now what? As we know, there is always travel distance between where you are and where you want to go. Now you need to take some actionable steps toward getting there so you can start to close the gap. As you begin to think about the necessary steps, you may run into challenges that feel like real problems. An essential skill for promoting your thriving and creating the future you want is knowing how to overcome obstacles that threaten to derail you from your goals.

Problems and obstacles are things that we don't want. From the FDT perspective, a guiding principle for overcoming any problem is to maximize the use of your limited resources, which include time, thought, and action, by allocating them toward obtaining what you do want. When we perceive a problem, it is very natural to focus on it; however, if we stay focused on the problem we don't want, that is where our resources get spent. The key to effective problem solving is to redirect your thinking as quickly as possible away from the problem and toward finding a solution. You can use the skills in this chapter to help you generate effective solutions to bring you closer to achieving your goals.

A SUCCESSFUL MIND-SET

As you start planning to achieve your goal, one of the best ways to prepare for potential obstacles is to adopt a successful mind-set. Failure is something you don't want; if you redirect all your thinking away from what you don't want and toward what you do want, you are left with success as the only option. Adopting the mind-set that success is the only option is not the same as believing you will not encounter obstacles — you surely will. What it means is that you will not allow any obstacle to deter you from what you want, and you will direct as many of your resources as possible toward your goal. You'll stay focused on your target and not entertain thoughts of failing. When you stay focused on success as the only option, then you have not spent any resources on overcoming obstacles in vain; all your actions, successful or not, are steps toward achieving your goals. Many very successful people have encountered obstacles and failures along the way to their success:

- Michael Jordan didn't make his high school basketball team. He was later named the greatest athlete of the twentieth century by ESPN.
- Ulysses S. Grant failed as a farmer, real estate agent, U.S. Customs official, and store clerk before becoming a general and later the president of the United States.
- Chicken Soup for the Soul was rejected by publishers a total of 123 times. The series now has sixty-five different titles and has sold more than 80 million copies all over the world.
- Walt Disney's first cartoon production company went bankrupt.
- John Grisham's first novel was rejected by sixteen agents and a dozen publishers. He later wrote several books that became bestsellers and were made into movies.
- The Beatles were rejected in 1962 by the Decca, Columbia, and HMV labels.
- Steven Spielberg was rejected from the University of Southern California's film school three times!

These incredibly successful people did not start out successful; rather, they were people who encountered failures and obstacles along the way to achieving what they wanted. What they all had in common was that they did not allow the obstacles to deter them. They kept going, no matter what.

Do this daily practice exercise to keep you in a successful frame of mind:

1. Think about your goal. (Read chapter 8 to create a SMART goal.)
2. Visualize it in your head. (Read chapter 9 to learn about how to create good visual simulations.)
3. Repeat out loud to yourself:
   "Success is the only option and I will find a way."
4. Say it again and again until you start to believe it.

Kate had a difficult relationship with her adult daughter. She felt that her daughter was caught up in a shallow Hollywood party lifestyle that was getting her nowhere, and they frequently argued about the choices her daughter was making. Kate set the goal of trying to repair the relationship with her daughter. She started with trying to be more understanding and less judgmental when they were talking on the phone. This seemed to go well, and after a few weeks they decided to meet for lunch — the first time in six months they had made a plan to see each other. Kate looked forward to it for an entire week and did lots of mental preparation and visualization to prime herself for having a good experience. But her daughter called the morning of their Sunday lunch date to cancel because she was not feeling well. Kate got upset and accused her daughter of partying too much and being hungover. Her daughter hung up on her, which left Kate fuming and frustrated. She felt she had tried a new mental approach and many new behaviors and done everything right, and she was angry that things hadn't gone as she had hoped. Her initial reaction was to throw in the towel and say, *See, I tried and it didn't work.*

After a few days, however, Kate found herself back in the place of wanting to repair the relationship. She knew there was no way she could give up on her own child, so she resolved that success was her only option. Now that she was feeling calmer, she was able to examine the situation to see what she could learn from it. She realized that she had jumped to conclusions and criticized her daughter, a pattern she was beginning to recognize. She saw that if she wanted to improve her relationship with her daughter she would need to learn to be more accepting and tolerant. Since her daughter was still not speaking to her, Kate decided to practice acceptance and tolerance with everyone else she encountered all day long. Within several days, Kate started to notice that when she focused on the positive qualities of others she automatically felt less critical and more accepting. She went home and made a long list of all the things she loved and appreciated about her daughter. Then she called her daughter and read the list to her voicemail. Two days later Kate got a tearful call from her daughter, and they had one of the most honest conversations they had had in years.

PLANNING

Now that you have established well-defined SMART goals based on your values statement, you will need to start planning how to turn a new goal into a real experience. Planning is the process of designing a set of integrated actions that, when carried out, will lead to accomplishing a specific goal. Good planning can prevent you from running into unanticipated obstacles, because it allows you to prepare for things you might encounter along the way.

Almost everything we do involves planning. We plan when and where we will have our next meal, what we will do during the day, and what we will wear. Though some people may feel they are not good at planning, the ability to plan is actually something all human beings possess.

Planning for a future goal usually requires that we set up many subgoals along the way. If you want to put dinner on the table at 6:00 PM and you don't have any food in the house, you will need to plan what to eat, when to go to the grocery store, and how much time you need to get there; you will need to buy the food and get back home in time to prepare the meal. Each of these steps along the way is a subgoal. Most of us plan on autopilot without even realizing that we are doing it. It is just a natural and necessary part of how we function in the world. Once you begin to harness the natural planning ability that we all have and direct it toward something you would like to achieve, you are well on the way toward deliberately creating your life.

BREAK IT DOWN INTO STEPS

The first thing to do in the planning process is to break things down into steps. Almost any task you start with can be broken down into smaller parts. Whether you are making dinner or trying to move to a new home, you can do only one thing at a time at any given moment. If you are feeling overwhelmed by a task, keep in mind that you only have to do one thing at a time, and eventually you will make progress. If you decided to walk from Los Angeles to New York, the task would seem daunting and probably undoable; but if you simply concentrated on putting one foot in front of the other, given enough time you would eventually get there.

The feeling of being overwhelmed is a very common reason for people to stop working on their goals. However, when you address each component of a problem individually, things don't seem so overwhelming. The easiest way to plan for success is to identify the small steps and stay focused on doing only one at a time at any given moment. If staying in the moment is a problem for you, work on the mindfulness exercises from chapter 6. When you stay in the moment and focus on just the step that is in your immediate now, almost anything is doable.

Choose one of your short-term goals from chapter 8, and see if you can identify the very first step you must take to accomplish it. For example:

Long-term goal: Get in better shape.
Short-term goal: Run two miles consecutively (this is what you are going to do).

If you get stuck, think about your goal and ask yourself the following three questions:

1. **When are you going to do it?**
   Literally, when? What day, what time of day? Make an appointment with yourself to achieve the steps of your goal.
   Monday, Wednesday, and Friday nights.
2. **Where are you going to do it?**
   Answering this question forces you to start visualizing it.
   I will go running on the treadmill at the gym.
3. **What are you going to need to do it?**
   What are the resources you need to make this happen? If you don't know, one of your very first subgoals will be to find out (read the section on exposure in chapter 9).
   Gym membership, running shoes and workout clothes, one hour of my time.

Once you have asked yourself these questions, you should have a pretty good idea of how to break your goal into subgoals. If you are using visualization, see yourself moving from wherever you are toward your goal. What order do the steps need to occur in? Create the first step, then the next step and the next, until you have identified all the steps necessary to get you there. There is no step too small. If your goal is to go to the gym, your goals might be: 1) picking out what you are going to wear, 2) putting the workout clothes on, 3) getting into your car, 4) driving to the gym, 5) parking your car, 6) walking into the gym, 7) using an exercise machine.

Visualize yourself accomplishing each of the steps before you attempt to do any of them. If you can see yourself accomplishing the task, you are well on your way to doing it. If at any point along the way you get stuck, stop and evaluate. What is coming up for you? Is it a feeling? Are you having an old limiting thought? Are you focusing on some aspect of the situation you don't want? Are you focused on the present step in the moment, or have you skipped ahead and let yourself become overwhelmed by the other steps? Are the steps too big? Can they be broken down further? If you find there is a step that you can't imagine, you might need more exposure to be able to visualize your goal in detail and to gather more information to help you discern the correct steps.

ASSESS THE CONSEQUENCES

As you plan the steps toward realizing your goal, you want to be able to anticipate the consequences of your actions. This requires extending your thoughts into the future and forming a hypothesis about what could happen. People who play chess are very good at this. They have to plan out in their minds the consequences of their moves and the moves of their opponent so that they can avoid losing their chess pieces. If the objective is to win the game (achieve your goal), you must think ahead. Everything you do in the present moment today affects what arrives in your present moment tomorrow.

As you map out the plan for achieving your goals, you will need to be able to anticipate whether the actions you are planning will really help you achieve them. If you want to become a financial success, you may need to anticipate the risk of playing the stock market versus putting your money into savings.

Often, assessing consequences will hinge on the reality of the present moment versus that of the faraway future goal. The present-moment choice may seem more tangible and perhaps more appealing. But when planning to achieve a future goal, we often don't get to do exactly what we want in the present moment; we defer it so that we can obtain delayed but more satisfying gratification later. When trying to lose weight, you give up eating the brownie now, but the delayed gratification is the much greater pleasure that you receive when you look in the mirror and see that you look great and have achieved your weight-loss goal. The further away the goal is, the more delayed gratification you will have to engage in. Most often you won't end up feeling good about an action that moves you further from your goal, no matter how good it feels in the moment. The brownie may be very tasty now, but how do you feel about it afterward? If you are filled with regret because it moved you away from your goal, was it really worth it? A good way to assess the consequences of a present action is to ask yourself:

ASK YOURSELF

Will I feel better or worse about myself afterward?

The actions you take in the present moment create the next present moment. You want everything you do to bring you closer to what you want in the future. The more time you spend creating subgoals with well-planned steps, the more vivid your goal will seem and the more you will be able to determine if your actions are consistent with your goal.

OVERCOMING OBSTACLES

Now that you have mapped out your plans, you will need to find solutions to obstacles that you still see getting in the way. The most common cause of failure for people trying to achieve goals is that they set up mental roadblocks. These *perceived* obstacles affect their ability to believe that what they want is possible. Many of these obstacles are fear based and come from focusing on unwanted aspects of the situation, such as the discomfort we feel when we think about doing something different and stepping outside our comfort zone. Other obstacles come from past experiences of failure that we use as evidence that we can't do something different. Some obstacles simply seem like undeniable facts. Every obstacle starts as a thought and leads to a feeling: *This is a very big project — I don't feel like I can really achieve that.* It is vital that you learn how to identify and get past these obstacles.

First, you need to identify the obstacles. Start with creating a list on the "Generating Solutions to Obstacles" worksheet on page 173. Write down everything you can think of that will get in the way. Don't censor yourself; just write down anything that comes to mind. Next, identify which problems feel like mental barriers, such as *I'm too old to go back to school*, and which feel like real ones, such as *I don't have enough money to buy the house I want*. A mental obstacle is likely to be more subjective, and you can probably find your own argument against it in your mind. But even if you logically know that it doesn't make sense, it keeps coming up, bringing with it enough emotion that it feels like a real barrier between you and your goal. Mental obstacles tend to come in the form of resistant thoughts, as discussed in chapter 5, and you can work on softening the resistance to mental barriers using some of the activities in that chapter. A real problem is more likely to be based on fact than on a mental obstacle, though there may be overlap at times. To get past what seem like real problems, you can try several different strategies.

CHECK YOUR ASSUMPTIONS

The first thing you should do when you bump up against what seems like a real problem is to determine whether you are making an assumption that arises from how you are looking at the situation. Many such assumptions will go unrecognized until you make a deliberate effort to identify them. Many assumptions that make a situation seem impossible are really just self-imposed limits or beliefs, and as we know, many of us hold beliefs that are not always based on reality.

For example, if you want a better-paying job, you might make some common assumptions, such as *To get a better-paying job I need more education, more experience, and different skills*. Once you have identified your assumptions about a situation, you need to check and challenge them. Are they really based on fact? See if you can come up with examples of situations in which your assumption may not be true. Are there other people with similar levels of skill and education who already have better-paying jobs? What about those Facebook guys? They don't even have college degrees. Okay, maybe that is an exceptional example, but there are likely to be more examples if you keep looking. If you start to find many examples that contradict your assumption, you can rethink whether you want to hold on to your assumption or let it go.

In some cases you may decide that even if your assumption isn't true across the board, it is actually appropriate for your situation. That is, many rather arbitrary assumptions and constraints are nevertheless desirable. For example, you may be able to get a better-paying job collecting garbage, but perhaps this isn't an option you are willing to consider, and more education and skills would help you get a better-paying job in a field of your choice. If you decide the assumption is based on fact — or is appropriate for your situation — you simply work with it and build it into your planning steps.

Below are some common assumptions that often come up as obstacles to goals. Check to see if any of these are coming up for you, then ask yourself the associated questions to assess the validity of your assumptions.

- **Time:** *I don't have enough time.* Are you doing other things with your time instead? Does the step really take as long as you think? Does it have to be done in the time period you have set for yourself?
- **Money:** *I don't have enough money.* Are there less expensive ways to do it? Can you find ways to raise more money? Can you get someone else to pay?
- **Cooperation:** *I don't have enough help.* Have you asked anyone for help? Whom have you asked? Have you really exhausted all the possibilities?
- **Culture:** *This is the way everyone else does it,* or *This is the way it has always been done.* But is it the way you want to do it? Does doing it this way work for you?

MANAGE YOUR RESOURCES

You may notice that some of the most common assumptions have to do with lacking resources, such as time, money, and help. People often limit themselves by believing they can't accomplish certain goals because they don't have the necessary resources. However, time, thought, and action are some of the most valuable resources in the process of creating your future, and they are available to everyone. If you think about something in the right way for long enough, there is almost no problem you can't solve. Time, conscious thought, and action, however, are all *limited* resources, and when you have a limited resource, you have to think about how you want to spend it, in the same way you might think about how you want to spend your money. The more of these resources you put toward your goals, the more likely you are to realize your dreams.

If you lack certain physical resources that you need, don't immediately rule out the goal if it is something you really want. For example, if you want to go back to college but don't have the money, acquiring the resources may become one of your short-term goals. Or you may need to expand your thought process to think of alternate ways to achieve your goals. Reexamine the underlying reasons you want to achieve that goal. Remember, if your reason is value driven, it is more about the feeling you get from achieving the goal than about the external representation. For example, if you value freedom, you might get that feeling from driving a fast red sports car, or you might get it from standing in an open field. Your goals should be representations of what you value formulated in ways that you believe you have the resources to achieve.

One of the biggest problems many people run into when they are trying to achieve new things is finding the time. *I want to go to the gym so I can get in shape, but I can't seem to find the time. I'd love to take a new dance class, but I'm too busy. I've always wanted to run a marathon, but finding time to train seems impossible.* Achieving anything that we want requires that we put forth the time and effort to make it happen. Thought and action both require time. Time is one of our most precious and limited resources, and how you spend it has a lot to do with what shows up in your life.

Ask Yourself

How much time per day am I willing to commit to thinking about my future, achieving my goals, and changing my life?

A well-established money-management concept that can also be used in the management of time is "Pay yourself first." This means that you should set aside time in your life to work on your goals and to make this a priority before you give time to anything or anyone else in your life. This may be a difficult concept for many people to absorb. Most people pay themselves *last* when it comes to the time they spend achieving their goals, putting everyone else's needs above their own. Keep in mind, however, that unless you set aside the necessary time, you will never be able to take the actions needed to create the life you want to live.

One of the first steps to managing your time is to become aware of how you use your time. Keeping an activity log, like the one at the end of this chapter, for one week can be a very useful and enlightening technique. While most people are aware of their general daily routines, many have never mapped out from day to night what they do with every hour of their day. Many people even find this to be a scary or even shameful thing to look at.

The goal of keeping a weekly activity log is awareness. Remember, without awareness there is no choice. Keep in mind that you can become aware of your behavior without judging or criticizing it. What you want to accomplish with your activity log is to 1) identify how you spend your time each day; 2) evaluate how you spend your time; and 3) make some active decisions about how you can increase the amount of time you spend on reaching your goals. Once you have assessed how you are spending your time, restructure your next week so that you are spending more of your time working toward a goal. Even if you find only one extra hour in your week, you'll be that much closer than if you don't use that hour. The more time you find, however, the sooner your goals will become present-moment experiences.

Jack had lots of goals but never felt he had the time to work on them. He had a busy schedule with a full-time job and three young children at home. Jack worried about the financial stability of his family. He knew that if he stayed in his current job, his annual raises would be minimal and he wouldn't be able to save enough money to send his kids to school. Jack had the goal to advance from accountant to certified financial planner so he could open his own business. In order to do so, he needed to take several courses and pass the licensing exam. Jack was motivated, but he felt overwhelmed and exhausted. He would come home from work at night, help the kids with their homework, and then crash in front of the TV to unwind for a few hours. The weekends seemed to fly by with chores and soccer games, and there just never seemed to be any extra time to enroll in the classes he needed. Jack realized he was on a treadmill to nowhere and that if something didn't change, in ten years his work situation would be exactly the same and the family's expenses would only increase.

Knowing he needed to find the extra time, Jack sat down with his wife and examined his schedule. He decided he would give up the one night a week he went bowling with his coworkers to enroll in an evening course at a community college; then he made an arrangement with his wife that Sunday afternoon would be his study time and she would take the kids out of the house to see her parents or go to the park. It would take about eighteen months for him to accomplish his goal this way, which seemed like a long haul, but he knew in the end it would get him to a better place financially, which was his ultimate goal.

Use the Power of Your Solution-Generating Mind

Let's review a few concepts. The brain is a solution-generating organism always trying to prepare you for anticipated future experiences. When you ask yourself a question, your mind goes to work to figure out how to answer it. Your brain has the ability to generate solutions to problems you don't even know exist yet. As we've discussed throughout this book, thoughts activate other similar thoughts. The more you think about something, the more ideas your brain will generate about it. One way to jump-start this natural solution-generating ability, in order to overcome obstacles, is to engage in brainstorming, which can be as simple as first writing the problem down and then writing down all the ideas that come to you. Make this an unfiltered list; don't rule any ideas out just because you don't think they are realistic. Continue with all the possible solutions you can think of. Later, come back and take a look at the list. Challenge your assumptions about the solutions that don't seem doable.

Remember that language-based thoughts, which happen on a conscious level, use only a small portion of our brain's thinking power. When generating solutions, we want to tap into as much of the brain's power as possible, including that which is stored unconsciously. If you do your brainstorming at night just before you go to bed, your brain will often work on the problem while you are asleep. You may even wake up in the middle of the night with a solution you hadn't thought of. Keep a pad of paper next to the bed so that if this happens you can write down whatever comes to mind. Einstein used this technique with good success, sometimes getting the "aha" while shaving the next morning. Another way to access unconscious forms of thinking is to phrase your problem as a question and then put yourself into a relaxed meditative state, either through the mindfulness and meditation techniques you have already learned or through activities such as self-hypnosis. When you open your eyes and bring yourself back to full consciousness, do your brainstorming, and your thoughts should flow more freely.

As you ponder the solution to your problem, keep in mind that your answer may come to you in the subtle form of your instinct or intuition. In other words, you may get a gut feeling about what you should do. Many people have difficulty trusting their instinct. They sometimes even believe that their internal voice is the source of their problems, so they learn to tune it out and instead listen to what other people tell them to do. People also sometimes confuse their thought process with their intuition. Thoughts we pay attention to and are aware of are happening at a language-based level, and we know that we make mistakes in this thinking process. While language-based thoughts are an interpretation of what our intuition is telling us, the larger part of intuition itself is happening at a much deeper sensory level, using many parts of the brain that do not communicate via language. Intuition, your instinctive gut reaction to a situation, can happen in the blink of an eye, as described in Malcolm Gladwell's book *Blink*.[1] Intuition gives you a wealth of information about what is in your best interests. If you have taught yourself to ignore or tune out your intuition, you can learn to tune back in by continuing to practice mindfulness and meditation, which will bring you more in touch with what is happening internally in the present moment.

CONSIDER POSSIBLE ALTERNATIVES

When mapping out your goals, you will eventually run into things over which you have little control. If your goal is to publish a book, at some point you have to deal with the issues of whether publishers like the book, whether they have a need for the type of book you have written, whether there is money in their budget to publish your book, and so on. It helps to practice being flexible and to begin thinking about possible alternatives to achieving your goal. In the case of writing a book, maybe self-publishing or creating an e-book is the way to go. In most cases, there are likely to be a number of alternatives you may not have considered.

If something out of your control is getting in the way of achieving your goal, you will need to think about the real reason you want to achieve your goal and what alternative goal you could create that would satisfy the same underlying purpose. For example, if your goal is to run a marathon but you tear a leg muscle, it may become very difficult to realistically achieve your stated goal. So take a look at why you wanted to achieve the goal in the first place. If fitness was one of the reasons you wanted to run a marathon, then perhaps swimming would be a perfectly acceptable and doable way to achieve the larger intention. Sometimes, when you consider other choices, you may even discover you like the other choice better, or you may discover something fun you hadn't tried before.

Being flexible is quite helpful not only in getting past obstacles but also in making decisions. Many people fear making decisions because they think that once they decide something they can never go back. While it would be nice if the decisions we made moved neatly from step to step, most of the time this isn't the case. We gather information all along the way in any decision-making process. New information may cause you to reassess the situation and change your mind. You may start a new job thinking it will be great, then meet your new boss and find out he is unbearable. Do you have to stay in the job? No! You can quit at any time. Or you may decide to try a solution to a problem that simply doesn't work. If you are lost in a city and you ask someone for directions, only to find that the person is just as lost as you, do you give up and remain lost? No! You simply ask someone else. Decision making is a flexible process. When you are flexible, you are able to respond to unintended consequences and remain open to new possibilities. You can make a decision and then change your mind or make a new decision at any point along the way.

Ask Someone Else

It goes without saying that you can only view a problem from your own perspective. In light of our discussion above of assumptions, it is easy to see how this can be limiting, especially if you are making assumptions you are not aware of. It can be very helpful to ask at least three people you trust for their opinions and/or advice. Often others can see things that are blocked from your view because of your own biases or blind spots. The key is to remember that they too are viewing the situation from their own perspective, so it helps to ask someone who has more experience or expertise than you do. It also helps to ask someone who is objective and not too invested in your goal. Remember, when asking others for their opinions, you are seeking information and ideas, not answers. Ultimately, you are the only person who knows your situation, so you will need to make choices that feel right for you — but having external input from the right people can provide you with valuable data for generating your own solutions.

Feedback and Reevaluation

As you bump up against obstacles on your journey, you can use what you learn along the way to obtain feedback and reevaluate. You may decide to go to graduate school to get a law degree, and then decide once you've taken a few classes that being a lawyer isn't for you. If you decide to drop out, this doesn't mean that you are a failure. What it means is that you learned something new along the way that you used as feedback to reevaluate your choice. You may have developed a new and stronger desire that is in conflict with your present destination. On any journey you will encounter lots of information along the way that you didn't have when you started out, information that you can use as feedback to reevaluate where you are. If you decide to drive from Los Angeles to San Francisco taking the I-5, but a twenty-car pileup closes the freeway before you get there, you will have to choose another route or pick a different destination.

This kind of thing happens all the time. We set out to go in one direction but something comes up that forces us to go in another. This doesn't mean we have to give up on what we want; it just means that our path might not be the one we first anticipated. Remember that if you are aware of the underlying reasons why you want something, you will often find many paths that can lead you there. Other times you may just find a preferable destination along the way that you didn't know existed before. Again, taking an alternate route or changing your destination doesn't mean you are giving up; it just means you are owning your freedom to alter your course at any time. It is what you learn along the way on any journey that helps guide your choices and prepares you for your ultimate destination.

Susie went to school to be a social worker. She was a thoughtful, kind person who loved helping people, and she thought it would be the perfect profession for putting her strengths to use. Soon after Susie began working for a county agency for child welfare, she found herself feeling very disturbed and having nightmares about her work. She felt as if what she had to offer was a drop in the bucket compared to the magnitude of the problems her clients struggled with. She felt that many families she tried to help were stuck in bad situations because there weren't enough resources being provided by the county, which made her feel powerless. After only a few months, Susie decided she wanted to make a bigger difference. She left her job as a social worker to take courses in fund-raising and business and eventually ended up leading a nonprofit organization that helped raise money for community volunteers and school programs.

WORKSHEET: GENERATING SOLUTIONS TO OBSTACLES

Write down the perceived real obstacles to your goal at the top of each column. Then ask yourself the solution-generating questions to see if you can find a way to overcome your obstacles.

Obstacles	1.	2.	3.
What are my assumptions? Are they based on fact?			
Am I managing my resources?			
Can I brainstorm any ideas?			
Is there an alternative way to achieve what I want?			
What do other people whom I trust think?			

Worksheet 10.1

From *Think Forward to Thrive* © 2014 by Jennice Vilhauer, PhD

Practice Assignments

1. Complete the "Generating Solutions to Obstacles" worksheet on page 173.
2. Complete the "How I Spend My Time" and "Self-Assessment of Time Management" worksheets on pages 175–176 and 177–178.
3. Now that you have assessed your weekly activities, use the "How I *Want* to Spend My Time" worksheet on pages 179–180, at the end of the chapter, to begin including more weekly activities that bring you closer to your life goals.

WORKSHEET: HOW I SPEND MY TIME

Write down your activities for each hour of the day. Place a check mark next to activities that you believe are necessary (n) in your life or helping you move toward your goals (g) and the things you want in life. If the activity fits into neither category, don't place a check mark in that box.

	Sunday	Monday	Tuesday	Wednesday	Thursday	Friday	Saturday
8:00 AM	n: ___ g: ___	n: ___ g: ___	n: ___ g: ___	n: ___ g: ___	n: ___ g: ___	n: ___ g: ___	n: ___ g: ___
9:00 AM	n: ___ g: ___	n: ___ g: ___	n: ___ g: ___	n: ___ g: ___	n: ___ g: ___	n: ___ g: ___	n: ___ g: ___
10:00 AM	n: ___ g: ___	n: ___ g: ___	n: ___ g: ___	n: ___ g: ___	n: ___ g: ___	n: ___ g: ___	n: ___ g: ___
11:00 AM	n: ___ g: ___	n: ___ g: ___	n: ___ g: ___	n: ___ g: ___	n: ___ g: ___	n: ___ g: ___	n: ___ g: ___
12:00 PM	n: ___ g: ___	n: ___ g: ___	n: ___ g: ___	n: ___ g: ___	n: ___ g: ___	n: ___ g: ___	n: ___ g: ___
1:00 PM	n: ___ g: ___	n: ___ g: ___	n: ___ g: ___	n: ___ g: ___	n: ___ g: ___	n: ___ g: ___	n: ___ g: ___
2:00 PM	n: ___ g: ___	n: ___ g: ___	n: ___ g: ___	n: ___ g: ___	n: ___ g: ___	n: ___ g: ___	n: ___ g: ___

Worksheet 10.2

	Sunday	Monday	Tuesday	Wednesday	Thursday	Friday	Saturday
3:00 PM	:____:00	:____:00	:____:00	:____:00	:____:00	:____:00	:____:00
4:00 PM	:____:00	:____:00	:____:00	:____:00	:____:00	:____:00	:____:00
5:00 PM	:____:00	:____:00	:____:00	:____:00	:____:00	:____:00	:____:00
6:00 PM	:____:00	:____:00	:____:00	:____:00	:____:00	:____:00	:____:00
7:00 PM	:____:00	:____:00	:____:00	:____:00	:____:00	:____:00	:____:00
8:00 PM	:____:00	:____:00	:____:00	:____:00	:____:00	:____:00	:____:00
9:00 PM	:____:00	:____:00	:____:00	:____:00	:____:00	:____:00	:____:00
10:00 PM	:____:00	:____:00	:____:00	:____:00	:____:00	:____:00	:____:00

Worksheet 10.2

From *Think Forward to Thrive* © 2014 by Jennice Vilhauer, PhD

WORKSHEET: SELF-ASSESSMENT OF TIME MANAGEMENT

1. Do I feel good in general about how I spend my time?

   _____

   _____

2. Do I spend any time during the week planning out how I want to spend my time, or does the way I spend my time happen by default?

   _____

   _____

3. Am I spending more time taking care of myself or taking care of other people?

   _____

   _____

4. What are my peak times of productivity?

   _____

   _____

5. What are the top three time wasters in my life?

   _____

   _____

6. Am I spending enough time working toward the things I want in life?

   _____

   _____

Worksheet 10.3   From *Think Forward to Thrive* © 2014 by Jennice Vilhauer, PhD

7. Are there things I am doing that aren't really necessary and don't move me toward my goals? If so, what are they?

_____

_____

8. Do I know how much time each week I should be spending on achieving my goals? If not, how can I find out? Have I set aside enough time to meet my goals?

_____

_____

9. When do I have the most flexibility — weekdays or weekends? Am I using my free time wisely?

_____

_____

10. Can I prioritize my activities to shift more of my time toward working on my goals? What activities can I move?

_____

_____

11. What is one thing I can change next week that will allow me to spend more time obtaining what I want?

_____

_____

Worksheet: How I Want to Spend My Time

Once you have evaluated your time management using the first log, use this one to write down your revised plan for each hour of the next week. Place a check mark next to activities that you believe are necessary (n) in your life or helping you move toward your goals (g) and the things you want in life. If the activity fits into neither category, don't place a check mark in that box.

	Sunday	Monday	Tuesday	Wednesday	Thursday	Friday	Saturday
8:00 AM	n:___ g:___	n:___ g:___	n:___ g:___	n:___ g:___	n:___ g:___	n:___ g:___	n:___ g:___
9:00 AM	n:___ g:___	n:___ g:___	n:___ g:___	n:___ g:___	n:___ g:___	n:___ g:___	n:___ g:___
10:00 AM	n:___ g:___	n:___ g:___	n:___ g:___	n:___ g:___	n:___ g:___	n:___ g:___	n:___ g:___
11:00 AM	n:___ g:___	n:___ g:___	n:___ g:___	n:___ g:___	n:___ g:___	n:___ g:___	n:___ g:___
12:00 PM	n:___ g:___	n:___ g:___	n:___ g:___	n:___ g:___	n:___ g:___	n:___ g:___	n:___ g:___
1:00 PM	n:___ g:___	n:___ g:___	n:___ g:___	n:___ g:___	n:___ g:___	n:___ g:___	n:___ g:___
2:00 PM	n:___ g:___	n:___ g:___	n:___ g:___	n:___ g:___	n:___ g:___	n:___ g:___	n:___ g:___

Worksheet 10.4

From *Think Forward to Thrive* © 2014 by Jennice Vilhauer, PhD

	Sunday	Monday	Tuesday	Wednesday	Thursday	Friday	Saturday
3:00 PM	__:__ to __:__	__:__ to __:__	__:__ to __:__	__:__ to __:__	__:__ to __:__	__:__ to __:__	__:__ to __:__
4:00 PM	__:__ to __:__	__:__ to __:__	__:__ to __:__	__:__ to __:__	__:__ to __:__	__:__ to __:__	__:__ to __:__
5:00 PM	__:__ to __:__	__:__ to __:__	__:__ to __:__	__:__ to __:__	__:__ to __:__	__:__ to __:__	__:__ to __:__
6:00 PM	__:__ to __:__	__:__ to __:__	__:__ to __:__	__:__ to __:__	__:__ to __:__	__:__ to __:__	__:__ to __:__
7:00 PM	__:__ to __:__	__:__ to __:__	__:__ to __:__	__:__ to __:__	__:__ to __:__	__:__ to __:__	__:__ to __:__
8:00 PM	__:__ to __:__	__:__ to __:__	__:__ to __:__	__:__ to __:__	__:__ to __:__	__:__ to __:__	__:__ to __:__
9:00 PM	__:__ to __:__	__:__ to __:__	__:__ to __:__	__:__ to __:__	__:__ to __:__	__:__ to __:__	__:__ to __:__
10:00 PM	__:__ to __:__	__:__ to __:__	__:__ to __:__	__:__ to __:__	__:__ to __:__	__:__ to __:__	__:__ to __:__

Worksheet 10.4

Tips for Thriving

- The key to effective problem solving is redirecting your thoughts as quickly as possible away from the problem and toward the solution and to use the skills you learned in this chapter to generate as many solutions as possible.

- One of the best ways to get around potential obstacles is to adopt a successful mind-set, before you even start planning toward your goals. You do this by making the commitment to yourself that *success is the only option*.

- Once you have a well-defined goal based on your values statement, you will need to start planning how to turn your new goal into a real experience.

- The first thing to do in the planning process is to break things down into steps. To do this, identify the first step you must take to accomplish your goal. If you get stuck, ask yourself these three questions:
    1. *When am I going to do it?*
    2. *Where am I going to do it?*
    3. *What am I going to need to do it?*

- As you are planning out the steps toward your goal, anticipate the potential consequences of your actions.

- The actions you take in the present moment create the next present moment. You want everything you do to bring you closer and closer to what you want in the future. When faced with any present-moment choice, assess whether the choice you are making is going to bring you closer to your goal or take you further away from it.

- Often, when you set a goal and start to make plans for how to achieve it, you bump up against obstacles. To overcome obstacles, try the following strategies:
    1. Check your assumptions.
    2. Manage your resources.
    3. Use the power of your solution-generating mind — ask yourself a question, and your mind will work on finding the answer.
    4. Consider possible alternatives.
    5. Ask someone else.

- Use feedback and reevaluation to assess your progress and make any necessary adjustments to your goals.

Chapter 11

TAKING ACTION

Small deeds done are better than great deeds planned.
—PETER MARSHALL

There is not one person on this planet who wouldn't choose to feel better or do better if he or she could. People who are not thriving don't know how to get past the barriers that keep them stuck. The biggest barrier of all is not taking action. People often say, *I know what to do; I just can't make myself do it.* What they don't realize is that not taking action is an action in itself. It is an action that maintains the status quo. If you're okay with that, great, but if you want to change your life you will have to do something different. There are no exceptions to this rule. Taking action is what changes your life; nothing else will ever accomplish this. All your good intentions and planning will not change your life until you actually take the actions necessary to make it happen. So what gets in the way?

OTHER BARRIERS TO ACTION

We have already discussed many of the barriers to action. The number one barrier is the expectation that something is not possible. Other barriers can make something that is possible seem undoable. These include feeling that the goal is not worth what it will cost to get there; focusing on what you don't want; using fear instead of hope as a motivator; holding onto old, competing beliefs; feeling that the task is too overwhelming; not recognizing that lack of action is consistent with a stored belief about yourself; and sometimes simply not knowing what the right steps are to achieve what you want. This chapter will teach you a new way to think about taking action by focusing on the benefits as opposed to the costs. It will also examine common barriers to action and help you identify how to bring yourself into a positive emotional state in which you are most likely to take action. Let's take a look at these other barriers one by one.

The Cost of the Action Seems Too High

Every action comes with a cost. We have to expend resources to take an action, whether it is the time to take the action, the thought we put into planning the necessary steps, the physical energy we need to execute the steps, or material resources such as money. We like to believe that taking an action will yield a result that is worth the resources expended. We are constantly assessing whether our actions will actually be worth the cost based on whether or not they move us in the direction of thriving. For example, if you want to win the lottery, you have to buy a ticket. But if you believe that the chances of winning are very low, you might not feel that the required resources — time to go get the ticket, money to buy the ticket, effort to physically go to the store rather than staying cozy at home — are worth expending. On the other hand, if you are already at the store and you see there is a big jackpot and all you have to do is spend a dollar, you might feel that the expenditure of resources is low enough to justify taking the action to purchase a ticket.

Because we have a drive toward thriving, instinctually we won't use our resources unless we are going to get something in return that benefits us, even if it is something as simple as a feeling we desire. Since resources help us to both survive and thrive, expending them without obtaining a return violates our basic nature. The cost of any action is generally something we don't want unless the perceived benefit, what we do want, is greater.

While this may make intuitive sense, here is where it gets tricky. Whether or not you think an action is worth taking often depends on where you are focusing your attention. We often make cost-benefit assessments so rapidly that we're not even aware that we are making them. Your brain does not have time to process every possible cost or benefit associated with a given situation; if our brains did that, we would never act on anything. So when your brain is on autopilot it takes a little shortcut; it uses the information that is most readily available to compute the cost-benefit equation. The available information is based on recent activity, determined by what you have been giving your attention to. It's almost as if your computer sorted all your files by those worked on in the past week, then used only those files to make rapid decisions, because that was all there was time to look through. It doesn't mean that other information isn't accessible; it just means it isn't being used because it isn't active.

We have discussed the fact that attention is a limited resource and that we prime ourselves to selectively filter information based on what we focus on. If you have been paying more attention to the costs of doing something, you are more likely to overestimate the cost, which may lead you to decide the action isn't worth it, even if it is something you would like to do. Exercise is a perfect example. Most people know that exercise has many wonderful benefits and would like to exercise more; however, many find that day after day they have a hard time getting themselves to do it. If you ask people with this goal how much they want to increase their exercise, they often will say *very much*. If you ask them how much they believe they could exercise more, most people will say that it is definitely in the realm of possibility. So what is the problem?

Well, the problem is very likely that at any given moment, when these people are making a decision about whether to exercise, they are focused on the cost or the resources they will have to expend, and they may even be focused on the benefits of not exercising. *I will have to put forth a lot of effort and I am tired, I will have to drive twenty minutes to get to the gym and twenty minutes to get back and spend at least an hour there, I don't have two extra hours in my day, I will have to give up the comfort of my couch, I will have to miss my favorite TV show, It is cold outside and I will have to endure an uncomfortable temperature, I hate the locker room at my gym, It always smells bad and I would prefer to avoid that.* If these thoughts continue day after day, week after week, then this is the information that is active in your brain in regards to whether or not to exercise. If this is the available information being processed, you can see why it would be easier to choose not to go to the gym.

Does this mean that other information is not accessible? No. You still have all the information you have ever taken in about the many benefits of exercise stored in your brain's memory. It just isn't being *automatically* accessed because it isn't as available due to lack of activity. If you want this information to be available to you when you are making choices, you need to activate it by consciously directing your attention to the benefits. If you do this regularly, the benefits will become the dominant thoughts on the subject, and they will be much more available to the automatic decision-making part of your brain. When you focus on how great the benefits of the action would be, the costs will likely no longer seem so large, and you may decide that taking the action really is worth it after all.

A simple way to consciously draw attention to a topic that you would like to activate in your brain is to keep a pad of paper next to your bed and write down as many benefits as you can think of in a given area where you would like to take action. Before you go to bed, read all the benefits; when you wake up in the morning, read the benefits again. Every night before you go to bed, add one new benefit to the list. It doesn't have to be something huge; it can be something like *If I exercise more I will look better in jeans* or *When I go to the gym I enjoy saying hello to the friendly people at the front desk.* It can really be anything that feels positive about the subject. Within just a few days these benefits will start to be more active in your brain, and you greatly increase the chances that you will take action. Remember, you want to look for opportunities to spend thought on the benefits of taking an action, so anything you can do during the day that actively draws attention to the benefits will help as well. Look up news articles or videos on the internet, talk about the benefits with your mate or your friends. The more you do, the more likely you are to act. If there is something you would like to do but are having a difficult time doing it, ask yourself:

ASK YOURSELF
Am I focusing on the cost or the benefits of the situation?

George had recently moved to Los Angeles from the Midwest to take a new job in computer engineering. He had always been somewhat shy; in a brand-new city he was finding it very difficult to make new friends, and as a result he was becoming increasingly isolated and anxious. George had difficulty initiating contact with people because he was fearful that people would think he wasn't very interesting compared to the glamorous people in the entertainment business, who seemed to be everywhere. When he thought about asking someone at work to lunch or talking to someone at the gym, he became paralyzed by the fear of rejection. George was so focused on what could go wrong and the cost of making a mistake that he began to think it simply wasn't worth it to try to make friends. Instead he stayed home most evenings alone. George had to refocus his attention on all the reasons why being social was important and worthwhile. At first this increased his anxiety a bit, because he started to realize that he very much wanted to make friends but was stuck feeling he didn't know how. This motivation, however, kept him focused on doing the things that would improve his situation, and he began to take more risks and step outside his comfort zone. He joined several Meetup groups as well as an online dating site.

On the next page you will find six steps to follow that will help you gain awareness of your process of deciding whether to take action. Use the six steps to walk through the "Six Steps to Action" worksheet on page 188. Notice whether you are more focused on the cost or the benefits of the situation. Spend some time really thinking about the benefits of the action, and see if that increases your motivation.

SIX STEPS TO ACTION

1. **What do you want?** Write down specifically what you are trying to achieve. What would you like to take action on?

2. **Why do you want to do it?** Think about the big picture here. If the action you are trying to take is going to the gym, but every time you think about going to the gym you find you don't want to expend the energy or leave the comfort of your home, the cost of going compared to the benefit of a single workout might seem low. On the other hand, if you are thinking of it as a step toward a much bigger goal you are trying to achieve, such as increasing your health and vitality and improving your quality of life, you may begin to realize that the cost is low in comparison to the real benefit.

3. **How much do you want it?** To answer this question, think about the specific activity in question 1 as well as the big-picture reason for engaging in the activity that you wrote down in question 2. Remember, it is your values that influence what you want.

4. **Do you believe it is possible?** Assess whether you think you can realistically take the action. This question isn't about thinking positively. Just saying that you believe something won't change the fact that you really don't. Use your instinct and emotion here. If you feel excited or confident, then you probably have a strong belief that it is possible. If you feel overwhelmed or the action seems like a fantasy, then you don't have a strong belief that it is possible.

5. **Is it worth it?** Here list the costs of taking the action and the benefits you would gain from the action. Remember that costs are resources such as time, money, effort, and thought, as well as giving up things that you enjoy. Use the lists that you generate to assess whether the actions seem worth the cost.

6. **Action.** When you have assessed that the cost would be worth the benefit, you now need to take a step forward. You don't have to do the whole thing at once. Remember that there are always steps toward anything you want to achieve. What is the first step? Try it. If it feels good, identify the next step and keep going.

Worksheet: Six Steps to Action

1. What do I want?

2. Why do I want it (big picture)?

3. How much do I want it?

0 1 2 3 4 5 6 7 8 9 10
Low   High

- Personal Values
- Societal Values

4. Do I believe it is possible?

0 1 2 3 4 5 6 7 8 9 10
Low   High

- Past Experience
- Other Learning

5. Is it worth it?

Cost (Don't want)	Benefits (Want)

0 1 2 3 4 5 6 7 8 9 10
No   Yes

Remember, if the benefits outweigh the cost, you must keep your thoughts focused on the benefits so that you can take action.

6. Action | **Take a step**

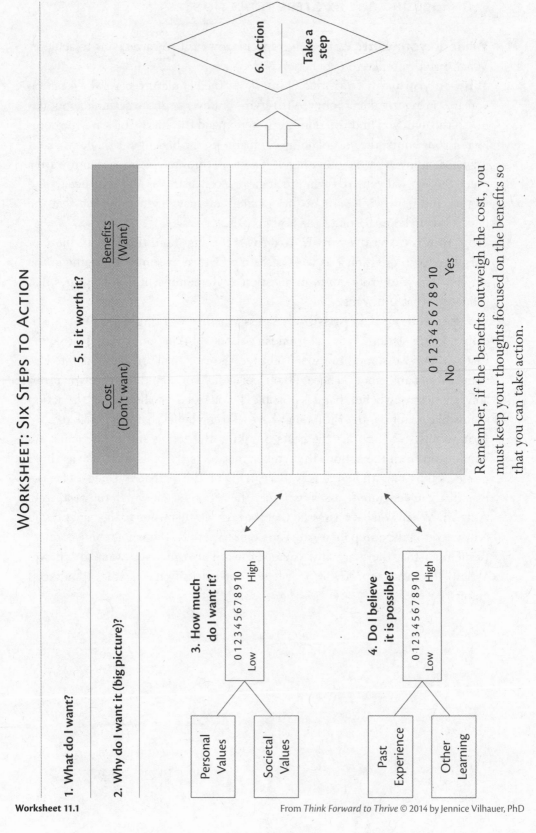

From *Think Forward to Thrive* © 2014 by Jennice Vilhauer, PhD

YOU ARE FOCUSING ON WHAT YOU DON'T WANT

When people identify something they want, they are almost always able to identify what they don't want as well. *I want more income but I don't want to pay more taxes. I want to get up early to exercise but I don't want to get out of bed.* Often what we do not want seems so undesirable that we spend a considerable amount of thought and energy figuring out how to avoid it, to the point where what we don't want becomes the basis of our actions.

When you take action based on what you don't want, you create a life that you don't want. If you start with the thought *I want a new relationship but I don't want to get rejected* and then focus on your fear of being rejected, you may make choices that prevent you from getting rejected, such as exiting a relationship at the slightest sign of something going wrong rather than working it out. Ultimately, choices based on what you *don't* want do not get you what you *do* want — in this example, a relationship.

> *When you take action based on what you don't want,*
> *you create a life that you don't want.*

YOU ARE FOCUSING ON THE BENEFIT OF *NOT* ACTING

Remember that the wanted and the unwanted always exist together. There are benefits to not taking action. *If I don't go to the gym I can stay home on the couch feeling comfortable and eat my favorite ice cream while I watch my favorite movie.* There is nothing wrong with this choice, but it won't get you closer to your goal of getting in shape and it may lead you to feeling worse later. Remember that delaying immediate gratification, thinking a bit further into the future, and making good choices in the present are all ways to invite what you want into your life. So how do you do this when your attention is completely absorbed by the benefits of *not* taking action toward your goals? The only answer to that question is that when you are consistently applying the tools you have learned in this book, the future you want will start to seem more real and therefore able to compete with what is happening in the present. As we know, when your future goals seem vague, far away, or unrealistic, your logical mind doesn't want to allocate resources to them. Being in shape just seems like a nice dream. However, when you have clearly defined goals that you visualize and meditate on every day, when you actively work on developing a plan and strategize to overcome the obstacles, your goal starts to seem very real and possible, and your brain starts to feel that allocating resources toward your goal makes sense.

YOU ARE RUNNING AWAY FROM YOUR FEAR

If you are having difficulty achieving a desired goal, you need to identify the primary motivating force behind your goal. If you are working toward something that will lead to thriving, it should feel good. But because of our faulty thinking, we often create goals that on the surface might seem great but that underneath cause us fear or anxiety, since we are busy thinking we might not achieve them.

When you run away from something instead of toward it, you focus on what you are running away from. Refocus your energy and thoughts on running toward your goal for the pure pleasure of achieving it. Your thought about your goal should be something like *I'm so excited about where I'm going because I will really enjoy being there.* If thinking about your goal is not bringing you a sense of pleasure, hope, happiness, or excitement but rather fear over what will happen if you don't achieve it, you need to reexamine whether it is a goal you truly want.

ASK YOURSELF

Why do I want the goal?
Am I being driven by fear or by hope?

OLD, COMPETING BELIEFS ARE GETTING IN THE WAY

When you decide to do something different, one of the most common barriers to action is your old belief system. As discussed, beliefs can exist both on an intellectual level and on a deeper, more emotional level. When you believe something only intellectually, you only partially believe it. Feelings are the indicator of your belief system. You must believe something very deeply for it to become something you really *feel* is true. Because many of our old beliefs have been around for a long time, they feel truer and we have stronger emotions associated with them. These old beliefs compete with the new beliefs and expectations you are trying to live by.

For example, if you have always been afraid of social interactions but you feel this fear has limited you and you would like to have more friends, then you may have identified an old belief, such as *I'm not good in social situations.* Your goal may be to replace this old belief with a new expectation, such as *There are many likeable things about me, and if I practice I can get over my shyness.* However, the old belief about not being good in social situations carries a good deal of associated emotion, such as anxiety and fear of rejection. Every time you encounter a social situation, it is likely that your old belief will trigger a strong emotional response. Simply repeating your new expectations to yourself may not be enough to overcome the emotions of the old belief.

The best way to get around old beliefs is to visualize the outcome of your new belief until you can actually feel what it would be like. While you can shift emotions rapidly, your body can't feel two competing emotions at once. It is impossible to feel relaxed and anxious at the same time. In the prior example, when you can picture yourself feeling happy or calm and relaxed in a social situation as well as how good it will feel to experience the positive social interaction, then you are far more likely to get beyond the old belief and take action consistent with the new belief you are working on.

You can start imagining what you want to feel in a given situation by picking a different situation in which the feeling comes more naturally. For example, if you want to feel calm at a party, picture yourself first feeling calm in an environment where calmness would come naturally to you, such as in a beautiful field of flowers. Close your eyes, imagine yourself sitting in the field, and stay there until you truly feel the sense of calm you are seeking (use your simulation skills from chapter 9). Once you can feel the calm in your body, bring the image of you at the party into your mind, and if you start to feel nervous, just go back to the field of flowers. Keep doing this until the calm feeling stays with you while you hold the image of the party in your mind.

The most limiting old belief you can have is *I can't*. Henry Ford wisely observed, "If you think you can or think you can't, you are right." As we know by now, no matter how much you want something, if you don't think you can achieve it, your brain simply won't want to put any resources toward accomplishing it. Remember that we act on what we expect or believe to be true, not on what we want. Be honest and ask yourself whether you really believe you can achieve your goal. If the answer is no, or if there is a significant amount of doubt, then that is why you are finding it so difficult to take action. Go back to chapter 5 and examine your resistance. Maybe the goal you've set for yourself is too big, or maybe you are stuck in an ineffective pattern of thinking.

NOT TAKING ACTION IS CONSISTENT WITH WHO YOU BELIEVE YOU ARE

We have seen many examples so far of how we create our future out of our stored beliefs. If you are carrying around the stored belief that you are *someone who doesn't accomplish things*, or *someone who can't do it alone*, or *someone who always fails at what you try*, then not taking action is simply the reality you are creating for yourself, consistent with what you believe about who you are. You will need to start with creating a new expectation about your ability to take action. Remember that creating a new expectation starts with a single thought. A thought does not become a belief until it is repeated over and over again and reinforced through action. The point is to reach for a thought that sounds more hopeful than where you started. If you can find a more hopeful thought, then you can turn it into a more deeply held belief. Remember, you shouldn't try to jump all the way up the continuum at once; work your way up slowly.

Fearful		Hopeful
X		X
I can't do it.	I can at least try.	I can do it.
I always fail.	*I have succeeded at some things.*	*There is no failure in life, only opportunities to learn.*

Once you have selected a more hopeful thought about your ability to take action, grow the thought with as much detail as possible. If you started with *I always fail*, and moved your way up to *I have succeeded at some things*, write a list as long as you can detailing everything you have ever succeeded at, even if it is as simple as getting up in the morning or reading this book. Keep repeating the new thought to yourself as often as you can, then see if you can take even a very small step toward the goal you are trying to work on.

YOU FEEL OVERWHELMED

Many people don't take action because they feel overwhelmed. This feeling of being overwhelmed usually comes from jumping too far ahead. The first strategy you should try when you are feeling overwhelmed is to use your mindfulness skills to stay focused on the present. Concentrating only on what is happening right in front of you will stop the flow of any negative thought projections. Additionally, staying in the present moment helps you gain the important awareness that you can only do one thing at a time. Many tasks seem overwhelming if you stop to think of the many steps it will take to get them done. However, if you simply focus on doing one thing at a time, you will begin to make progress.

To pull back into the present moment, try one of the mindfulness exercises from chapter 6. When you are feeling calmer, check your thoughts to see which ones are creating this negative emotion, then see if you can replace those thoughts with new ones that move you up the emotional continuum. If you are having difficulty finding the old thought or coming up with one on your own, try something like *I don't have to do it all at once — I can break it down into doable steps*. Once you have come up with a new thought that allows you to feel calmer, see if you can employ some of the strategies outlined in chapter 10 to help with breaking the task down until it starts to feel more manageable.

YOU DON'T KNOW HOW

Sometimes we decide we want something but we don't know how to get it, so we don't do anything at all. Instead of giving in to feeling helpless (a negative future projection that you can't make it happen), make it your goal or action task to find out how you *can* make it happen.

As you know, the less exposure you have to something, the less clear the necessary steps will be. Just because the steps are not obvious, though, doesn't mean you don't have the resources or ability to figure out what they are. The more you expose yourself to what you want, the more real it will seem and the more ideas will come to you about how to make it happen. In the process, you will start to believe more and more that achieving what you want is possible, and you will be more likely to take action. Remember, if you participate in the process and follow the threads that feel good, the answers will start to unfold.

YOU CAN'T IDENTIFY THE BARRIER

It is often difficult to see our own behavior as clearly as someone else might see it. If you've been working toward something without results, and even after reading this chapter you can't identify what the barrier to success might be, it is likely that the barrier is in your personal blind spot and you will need the help of another person to see it. This other person could be a trusted family member, a close friend, or a trained behavioral professional such as a psychologist who can work with you one-on-one to help identify the barriers. Don't be afraid to ask for help.

EMOTIONAL ALIGNMENT FOR POSITIVE ACTION

You may be taking actions toward what you want and still finding that things just don't seem to be working. It feels like no matter what you do, it isn't getting you anywhere, or at best it feels like a lot of very effortful work. This is because there is more than one way to do something, and you may not be approaching your goal in the optimal way. Imagine there is a heavy tire on your front lawn that you want to move into the garage. If you drag the tire there, it will take a lot of effort; if you roll it there, it will feel much easier. Either way you'll get it there, but one way is much more difficult and less pleasurable than the other.

When you are out of emotional alignment with what you are doing, it will feel like dragging the tire instead of rolling it. If you are taking actions toward what you want in life but it doesn't feel good — it just feels like a lot of work — chances are you are out of emotional alignment with your goal but still taking action because you believe you should. For example, if you choose to eat a salad for lunch but you spend the whole time thinking about the really delicious pizza you had to give up, you're going to find eating the salad effortful and unpleasant. Trying to maintain a goal of healthy eating will be very painful and difficult if you go about it this way. It would be better to stop what you are doing and try to align your emotions with your goal by refocusing on the benefits of taking the action. Spending five minutes to refocus on the wanted aspects of any situation and reminding yourself why you are expending effort on it is worth its weight in gold. For example, if before lunch you had spent five minutes visualizing what you would look and feel like, how much energy you'd have, what kinds of clothes you would buy, and how many compliments you would get after you had maintained your healthy eating habits for a while, you would be feeling good about your goal, so you would be in emotional alignment with it as you chose from the menu. The salad will taste much better, and you will feel much better about your choice since you focused on the benefits of your goal and not on the cost of eating the salad. It is the difference between rolling the tire and dragging it. When you find yourself taking action but it feels very difficult, stop and ask yourself:

ASK YOURSELF

Am I dragging the tire or rolling it?

Being in emotional alignment before you take action is a great way to get the most from the resources you are spending. Your actions will feel totally different to you and you'll be more likely to continue with them. Even if you are trying to accomplish something that is not necessarily goal specific, it is easier to take action on almost anything when you are in a positive emotional state. We tend to think more clearly when we are feeling positive, and therefore we experience less internal resistance. If you know you need to accomplish something difficult or something that you have been putting off, try to approach it from the most positive mental state possible. Below is an activity that can help elevate your mood and point you in the right direction.

EMOTIONAL ALIGNMENT EXERCISE

This exercise combines mindfulness, meditation, and visualization to help bring you into the right frame of mind for taking action.

- Reduce the stimulation in your environment. Go to a room by yourself; turn off the TV, the lights, the radio, and the phone; if you don't live by yourself and you don't have your own room, go sit in your car, the bathroom, or even a closet.
- Put on relaxing music.

- Light a candle.
- Sit quietly in a chair with your eyes closed.
- Try to bring yourself into the present moment by focusing on your breathing.
- See if you can visualize yourself already having completed the action you are trying to take.
- See and feel yourself enjoying all the benefits of having taken the action.

DON'T WAIT TO FEEL MOTIVATED

While it is best to feel emotionally aligned with your goals, if you've been feeling down or depressed for a long time and you haven't taken action toward something you want because you are waiting until you feel like doing it, be aware that that feeling may never come — until you take the action. You must keep in mind that behavior and emotion are two different things — you can act differently than you feel. While we often have an emotion and then take an action accordingly, like feeling sad and then staying home in bed, the process can work in reverse too. You can take an action and let the feeling follow. You can go visit a friend and feel happy about connecting. You can clean your house and feel proud of your accomplishment. Knowing that you want to do something because it brings you closer to your goal is enough reason to take action, even if you don't feel like it in the moment.

CONSISTENCY AND COMMITMENT

One of the most self-defeating thoughts you can have is *Because I haven't succeeded in the past, I won't succeed in the future.* This is simply another version of believing it isn't possible, another negative future projection. The past does not dictate the future. Just because you have never done it before does not mean that you can't start now and change your future. As the wise saying goes, *While it might feel easier to do what you have always done, if you are not happy with what you have always gotten, then you will have to do something different.*

Moving to a place of well-being in your life simply requires consistency and commitment. Remember the scenario of walking from Los Angeles to New York — if you just put one foot in front of the other you will get there eventually. If you do even one small thing toward your goal every day, you will get closer and closer to it. If you aren't able to do something every day, then commit to as much effort as you feel is reasonable; just remember that the more you do, the closer you get to achieving your goals. Keep in mind that living well is a skill and, like any other skill, it takes consistent practice to improve at and eventually master it.

PRACTICE ASSIGNMENTS

1. Pick an area of your life in which you have been struggling to take action. Complete the "Six Steps to Action" worksheet on page 188.
2. Next time you feel stuck, use the positive emotional alignment activity in this chapter to refocus on the benefits you get from taking the action, and put yourself in the right frame of mind.

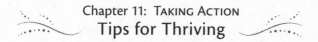
Tips for Thriving

- If you want to change your life in any way, you will have to do something different. There are no exceptions to this rule.
- Some common barriers to action include:
    - The cost of the action seems too high, because you are focused primarily on the costs and not the benefits. Refocus your attention on the benefits of the action, and see if that shifts your motivation to take action.
    - You're focusing on what you don't want instead of what you do want. If you allocate more thoughts to what you do want than to what you don't, you are far more likely to take action.
    - Old, competing beliefs are getting in the way of taking action on a new way of thinking. Perhaps you tried to leap too far with your new goal, and now you're encountering resistance. Adjust your goal until it represents improvement but still feels believable.
    - You're feeling overwhelmed, which stops you from taking action. Just remember, you can only do one thing at a time in any given moment, and if you break goals down into small enough steps, you can accomplish anything.
    - You don't know how. Sometimes the biggest part of doing anything new is learning how. Educating yourself simply becomes part of the goal, another step toward where you want to be.
- If you take action while you are in emotional alignment with your goal, your actions will take less effort, and you will feel like you are getting more out of what you are doing.
- Don't wait to feel motivated to take action; often the feeling follows the action.
- If you do anything, no matter how small, with consistency and commitment, you will eventually see change.

Chapter 12

ALLOWING THE FUTURE TO ARRIVE

For time and the world do not stand still. Change is the law of life.
——JOHN F. KENNEDY

The essence of life is change. With every moment that flows by, we gradually become someone different, and we can never return to being who we were. The only reason you can look back is that you've come so far. The present is where the power to change your life lies, but you cannot hold on to the present moment; it continually gives way to the future. The future will arrive whether or not you are ready for it, but you do have a choice in how you greet it. You can resist it, or you can embrace its arrival.

When you embrace the future, you choose to view everything you encounter as an opportunity for growth. As you begin to consciously engage in change, you will come across challenges along the way; if you embrace them, the challenges can teach you who you are and how to identify what you want, make you more aware of what you need to do, and help you develop the strength to build the life you desire. Consider the arrival of the future a constant stream of gifts coming into your life, giving you the chance to learn what you need to know in order to thrive. When things enter your experience that you don't like, view them as opportunities to clarify even more strongly what you do want and to renew your commitment to work toward it. When you start to feel overwhelmed, view it as an opportunity to adjust your thinking and to gain greater control over your mind. When things go wrong, use it as an opportunity to be thankful for all the things that go right and focus appreciatively on those things. If you embrace these opportunities, you embrace changing for the better.

Many of us don't realize that we can't attain what we want without the challenges that prepare us along the way. We all want to have good relationships, but sometimes we need to have difficult ones to show us what areas we still need to grow in. When butterflies emerge from their cocoons, they struggle, sometimes violently, to break free. If you help the butterfly out of its cocoon, it will not build the strength in its wings that it needs to fly away; instead, it will die. If you let it struggle through the challenge, it will become strong enough to fly away freely.

Often instead of embracing the challenges that make us stronger and bring us closer to our goal, we give up in frustration — or we never even bother to try — not realizing that by not taking action toward something we want, we are taking action *against* it. You may want vibrant health, but you won't get it sitting on the couch watching TV every day. You'll get it by eating well, exercising, and taking care of your emotional well-being. When you do these things consistently, health begins to arrive in your present moment. The challenges we encounter are all opportunities for a better future if we embrace them.

The future will arrive whether or not you are ready for it,
but you do have a choice in how you greet it.

Let Go of Resistance

Resistance often comes from fighting experiences that we don't like. We get angry, upset, indignant, or frustrated at how unfair life seems. However, the more we fight, the worse we feel. Fighting these experiences focuses our attention on them, and we know that what you give your attention to only grows bigger.

The situations we encounter help us define what we want and show us what direction we should be moving in. Sickness can help clarify our desire for health, since it motivates us to seek more knowledge and to take actions that lead to health. A bad relationship can help you clarify what you want in a good relationship, such as understanding and shared purpose, so that you will seek those things out with your next partner. If you focus on what the experience is showing you and use it as a guide to learn about your preferences and to motivate you toward action, then you are embracing the experience. If instead you dwell on all the reasons you dislike the experience or insist on believing the experience is unfair, then you are resisting what the experience has to offer you.

In order to let go of resistance, you must first identify it. This is the easy part — your emotions will always tell you. Negative emotions, such as anxiety or anger, are almost always a sign of resisting rather than embracing an experience. When you identify a negative emotion about an experience, try to identify what aspect of the situation is causing the emotion, or what specifically it is that you don't like. Then, instead of stopping there and focusing on what's wrong, which is what many people do, direct your attention away from it by focusing on the improvement you want instead. Focus your energy on how good that would feel, so that you can use your dislike of the present situation to motivate you to take action toward what you prefer. Remember, if you don't like the present moment, that's okay, because by the time you think of it, it is already gone. Something new keeps arriving every moment, and you have the power to shape those moments.

BE WILLING TO CHANGE

If you want to change something in your life, you must first realize that change has to take place within you. It is often easier to believe that our distress is due to the other people in our lives, or to events and circumstances. As you have learned from reading this book, however, it is our own thoughts and actions that create the majority of our experiences in every moment.

You must be willing to start wherever you are, no matter how bad you feel, and do the things you know how to do and practice the skills you have learned, whether or not you feel like it. There will be many days when the future you want seems too far away to work toward it. However, without your commitment to change in the present moment, a better future will never arrive. Remember that you don't have to change all at once, but you must commit to shifting your thoughts in a direction that leads to feeling better. As you have learned, your emotions will always guide you. Even when the emotional shift seems slow and every action feels painful, remember that there are only two directions you can go in life — away from what you want or toward it. The simple willingness to change no matter where you are points you toward your better future.

FIGHT FOR THE RIGHT TO LIVE WELL

Living well is a subjective state, but when you feel emotionally well and balanced, you are moving toward a state of thriving, and more of what you want will begin to arrive in your life. Anything short of that, and you are moving away from thriving. Protecting and defending your right to thrive should be your highest priority. That means taking the best care of yourself you can and not allowing people or situations to pull you away from your own well-being. If someone in your life does not support your choice to live well, then keep moving away from that person until his or her influence does not affect you.

Often the greatest obstacle to living well is us. We spend lots of time arguing for our limitations and the reasons why we can't do the things we know we could be doing to promote our thriving. *I am sick, I am depressed, I don't have enough energy, I had lousy parents, My spouse doesn't love me, I don't have enough money or time* — these are just a few examples of perceived limitations that stop many people from thriving. While these things may or may not be true, they can turn into excuses people make for focusing on what they can't do instead of on what they can do. Even the sickest person can focus on his or her remaining health.

When you argue for your limitations, you simply make them bigger and more entrenched in your belief system. Often people hide behind their limitations because the thought of taking responsibility for their thriving is too daunting. This thinking is largely driven by the fear that if they do not succeed, it will be their fault.

Controlling your ability to thrive in life is far more empowering than believing your success is up to someone else or subject to random circumstances. Realize that the courage to try is a success all by itself. There is no arbitrary standard that you have to measure up to and no place that you have to go. It is impossible to do it all. The goal is really just to thrive, have fun, and enjoy whatever you decide to do.

LIVE READY!

People often make the mistake of believing that if the good things in their lives would just show up, then they could be happy and things would change. *If I had a job, then I would have a reason to get off the couch and stop watching TV all day.* The problem with this line of thinking is that if you are sitting on the couch all day, the job you want will never show up. We get things in life that we "match up" with. Someone with a great job showed up ready for the job. Such people likely worked hard, identified the skills that were needed, gained experience, built their résumés, polished their interview skills, paid careful attention to how they were being perceived, and gave potential employers exactly what they were looking for. It didn't just happen; they weren't just lucky. They wanted it and were ready for the opportunity when it arrived.

Most people live ready for what they expect in life, not for what they want. If you want a great partner but never expect to meet anyone, then chances are that half the time when you leave the house, you never even think about what you look like. If, however, you expected to meet your great new partner at any moment, you would probably pay more attention to your appearance even when just going out for a gallon of milk. If you felt great about yourself every time you left the house, you would be more likely to give off great energy and also more likely to talk to others, which would greatly increase the chances of meeting someone.

Living ready means living as if the things you want are coming at any moment. This has two huge benefits. First, when an opportunity shows up, you are ready to take advantage of it. Second, when you live as if what you want is coming, your belief that it will occur starts to grow very rapidly and you start to engage in more and more actions likely to make it happen. As you begin to change your present moment by living ready, you automatically change the future that will arrive.

*Living ready means living as if the things
you want are coming at any moment.*

DEAL WITH DISAPPOINTMENT

Many people "hope for the best but expect the worst," as the saying goes, because they fear disappointment. Disappointment is difficult to tolerate for various reasons, depending on the person. Some people assume that if they don't get what they want, then their belief that they aren't good enough and that they will never achieve their goals has been confirmed. Remember, we look for information in our environment to confirm what we already believe. But those beliefs don't serve you and certainly don't point you in the direction of thriving; they just make you feel bad. Also, remember that action is directly related to expectation. If you are putting energy into preparing for the worst, then that is energy you are not directing toward what you want, and if you don't really expect the best, then chances are you are not doing everything you can to make it happen.

Disappointment is not the result of a situation but rather of how you frame the situation. If you take not getting something you want to mean something negative about who you are, then you will end up feeling bad. If instead you take it as an opportunity to learn about how to better prepare for what you want, then every opportunity becomes something to be thankful for.

When you don't get what you want in life, instead of feeling disappointed, use it as an opportunity to ask yourself:

ASK YOURSELF

*Was I really prepared? Did I really believe it was possible?
Did I take all the actions necessary to make it happen?
Can I learn something from this situation
that will help me be more prepared?*

POTHOLES IN THE ROAD

As you move along the road toward well-being and thriving, you are likely to hit a few potholes along the way. You might be doing all the things you know to do to take care of yourself, starting to feel good, and seeing progress in your life, and then all of a sudden something comes along that completely throws you and you feel like you're right back to where you started.

The good news is you can't ever go all the way back. It is like riding a bike — once you learn, you never forget how. You might crash, get a few bruises, and feel some pain, but you never forget how to ride the bike. You can get back up at any time and start riding again. We all have sensitive spots, and when they get hit, a flood of negative emotions can be triggered. These trigger areas are generally related to very deeply held and often painful beliefs about ourselves. *I'm not good enough, I'm unworthy, I'm unlovable, I'm incapable and useless.* People sometimes develop very unhealthy ways to cope with these deeply held beliefs, such as drinking and doing drugs, shopping excessively, getting into codependent relationships, overeating, thinking about suicide, or other self-harming behaviors. These sensitive spots and our attempts to cope with them are the source of most potholes on the road to well-being. Many situations can trigger your sensitive spots, and it's difficult to always be prepared for them. You can, however, pay attention to the signs indicating a potential pothole ahead.

- **You start slacking off on the things that make you feel good.** Maybe you stop eating healthfully, spend less time with friends, exercise or meditate less, stop reading helpful books, stop listening to inspirational music, or stop nurturing yourself as much as you know you should.
- **You experience an increase in negative emotions.** The more you start to feel better, the more sensitive you will become to feeling bad. When you sense a negative emotion of any kind, don't simply ignore it; try to identify the source and take action toward feeling better.
- **You put yourself in situations that you know trigger your sensitive spots.** You may start to engage in risky behaviors, such as agreeing to get together with the abusive ex-boyfriend, hanging out with friends who use drugs even though you are trying to stay sober, spending too much time with people who are always negative, buying a giant box of doughnuts and telling yourself you will only eat one. People tend to place themselves in these situations when they haven't yet started to feel the real, lasting benefits of being on the road to well-being and are missing the temporary feel-good effects from their old ways of coping.

When you find yourself in a pothole, the fastest way to get out of it is to do what you know works, then do more and more of it. If meditation helps you feel calm, then instead of meditating for the usual fifteen minutes, meditate for an hour or more; if exercise calms you, then exercise twice a day; if taking a bubble bath makes you feel better, take one every night. Unfortunately, when many people fall into a pothole, they do the opposite — they immediately stop doing all the things they know could help them. The most important thing is to pull yourself out as soon as you can. Though we're using the metaphor of a pothole, the reality is that when you get dragged down by negative emotions and self-defeating behaviors, you don't just get stuck in one spot on the road; you move yourself further away from your goal. Eating a box of doughnuts doesn't just keep you from losing weight; it makes you gain weight. As stated many times in this book, you can only go in two directions in life — toward thriving or away from it. When you are stuck in a place of negative emotions, those feelings quickly lead to actions that take you further and further away from where you want to go. Fortunately, you can use many of the tools in this book to pull yourself out of a pothole; simply rereading a chapter or two can put you back on track.

When you find yourself in a pothole, the fastest way to get out of it is to do what you know works, then do more and more of it.

CREATING YOUR LIGHT AT THE END OF THE TUNNEL

By now you have learned many skills to help you create your desired future. Keep in mind that you can use these skills to improve your life, and to create a light at the end of the tunnel, in almost any situation, whether the better future you want is five minutes away, five days away, or five years away. The "Changing Distress into Success" exercise at the end of chapter 4 can be a very helpful tool if you are in the middle of an immediate crisis or if you are worried about something in the near future. Regardless of your situation, start the process with the present moment and ask yourself the single most important question: *What do I want?* You can use any variation that helps you identify the improved future you are seeking, such as *Where do I want to go? How do I want this situation to turn out?* If you are having trouble figuring that out, go back to chapter 8 and read the section on identifying what you want. As you recall, it is often easiest to start by identifying what you don't want or don't like about the situation and then turn it around to the find the flip side. If you know you don't like where you live, write down what you don't like about it — maybe it's too small and noisy. Now you can see, from a *presence* of perspective, that what you want is a larger, quieter space. This gives you a place to start. Now that you have what you want in your mind and a direction for where you want to go, you can grow this into something more specific by continuing to focus on it.

As you know so well by now, when you pay attention to what you want, your mind will begin to work on how to get you there. Even if you have no idea where to start, as long as you participate in the process and follow any thread, doing anything you know to do in pursuit of what you want, you will begin to obtain new information that will open up opportunities that you didn't even know existed.

When in doubt, do lots of internet searches, read books on the subject, and talk about what you want with everyone you know. It is amazing how much information these activities can yield. The problem-solving center of your brain will work with this new information to generate solutions that will arrive in your mind as new ideas, things you hadn't thought of before.

If you are doubting yourself and don't feel you can achieve what you want, you can go back to chapter 4 and see if you might not be limiting yourself with old beliefs. Or perhaps you have made too large a leap and you will need to scale back until what you want feels doable. Remember, from wherever you are, you are reaching for an improvement; you don't have to go all the way in the first try. Once you know that what you want is aligned with your values, and feel a fair degree of confidence that it is within your ability to achieve, you can turn what you want into a concrete goal by reviewing the steps in chapter 8. Once you have a SMART goal in mind, you will want to make your goal as tangible as possible by visualizing yourself actually achieving the goal. Remember from chapter 9 that the more real you make your visual simulations by integrating as much sensory data as possible, and the more time you spend visualizing, the more your brain will help you prepare for the arrival of your desired future. Don't forget that when doing visualization, it is best to do both outcome simulations, in which you see yourself having achieved the goal, and process simulations, in which you see yourself taking the necessary steps to get there.

If, as you prepare to start taking actions toward your goal, you bump up against real problems along the way, review chapter 10 for ways to generate solutions. If you are having difficulty taking action, chapter 11 can help you evaluate whether you are focused on the cost or the benefits of taking the action. See if really giving your attention to the benefits helps you gain motivation to get going. If not, look at some of the other common barriers to action and see if they may apply to your situation. If at any point in this process you start to have doubting or resistant thoughts about what you are trying to achieve, don't just ignore them. Go back to chapter 5 and see if you can use some of the exercises there to reduce the resistance or break away from ineffective patterns of thinking that may be keeping you stuck.

Most important to your success as you make your way toward the light at the end of the tunnel is staying the course. You may feel at times that your efforts are getting you nowhere — but the skills you have learned in this book can move you in a better direction if you practice them consistently. On your journey an element of faith will at times be required because you won't be able to see the destination. You will need to trust that as you participate in the process the path will continue to unfold. Also, keep in mind there will be places along the way that you don't like; don't use them as a reason to turn around. If you get to one of these places, close your eyes, visualize the outcome simulation you've created, and repeat to yourself over and over, until the urge to turn around passes, "Success is the only option, and I will find a way."

After almost twelve years of practicing as a psychologist and five years of using the skills outlined in this book with patients, I can say that those who do the work benefit and achieve a positive sense of thriving that many say they have never felt before. Nothing in this book is a magical solution; reading the chapters will provide you with new knowledge, but you must engage in the process and the activities in order to achieve the change you are seeking. A large number of people who have participated in the Future Directed Therapy course started off as disbelievers; they had heard it or tried it all before. To some the skills sounded too simplistic to help with their big problems, others felt they "understood" the material so they thought that meant if their life hadn't changed it didn't work, while others stated when they tried some of the skills it just felt unnatural. The single common denominator for those who achieved the improvements they were seeking was that they did the work. It wasn't easy. Some people reported they had to read the book three times before they recognized they were not actually *doing* the work. But those who followed the steps and participated in the process often reported not only being pleased but truly surprised by the changes and the amount of growth that occurred in their lives. Experience is the truest teacher, but in order to experience you must do. If you have read this far and you are still struggling, stop, close your eyes, and ask yourself:

◢ ASK YOURSELF

Do I want change badly enough to do the work?

THERE IS BEAUTY IN BAKERSFIELD

Many people become frustrated when they feel they have not yet arrived where they are trying to go. They mistakenly believe that they cannot be happy until they get there. It is the journey, however, that allows you to become the person you aspire to be. Every place you encounter between where you are and where you want to go can provide you with an opportunity that will slowly transform you along the way. Remember that what you see is largely about what you look for. Even Bakersfield can be beautiful if you look at it the right way. If you reach a place where you don't want to be, remember that the wanted and the unwanted always exist together. Look for the opportunities that are present to help you along. Just like the butterfly emerging from its cocoon, you need the struggles to help you become strong enough to reach your destination.

You Are the Creator of Your Future Life

Your future life is arriving every moment, and most of what arrives is not an acci-dent. While it may be a bit daunting to realize that you are responsible for the life you create, it should also be empowering to know that you alone hold the power to change the future. If you feel bad, you are the one who can shift your thoughts toward feeling better. If you are dissatisfied with your life, you are the one who can change your actions to create more fulfilling experiences. Remember that every-thing you do matters and that every action you take creates the next present moment. Life is a gift, and what you do with it is up to you. You now have the awareness to make a choice.

Live well and thrive!

PRACTICE ASSIGNMENTS

1. Read this book again, then read it again. And again! Every time you read it you will retain something new. Remember, you are constantly in a state of change. Each time you read the book you will be in a different place than you were the last time you read it, and the information will take on a new and deeper meaning every time. Guaranteed!

2. Do each of the practice assignments again and keep doing them until you start to feel better.

3. To find out more about Future Directed Therapy, or to find a professional trained in FDT who can work with you on these skills, please go to www.FutureDirectedTherapy.com.

- The future will arrive whether or not you are ready for it, but you do have a choice in how you greet it. You can resist the future, or you can embrace it.

- Let go of resistance by redirecting your attention away from the unwanted aspect of the situation. See if you can focus on what you would like to have happen instead.

- View every moment and every experience as an opportunity, not an opposition.

- Be willing to change. You must be ready to start wherever you are, no matter how bad you feel, and to do the things you know how to do and practice the skills you have learned, whether or not you feel like it.

- Fight for the right to live well instead of arguing for your limitations. Every bit of energy that you invest in arguing for why you can't do something is energy that you aren't investing in accomplishing what you want.

- Live ready. Live as if the things you want are coming at any moment. When they show up, you will be prepared, and you won't miss out on an opportunity.

- Deal with disappointment. Disappointment is not the result of a situation but rather of how you frame the situation. Use disappointments as opportunities to learn about how to get better prepared for the future you desire.

- On the road to well-being there will always be potholes. There are usually signs that a pothole is ahead, and it is best to heed these signs; however, when you do find yourself in a pothole, the fastest way to get out of it is to do what you know works to make you feel better, then do more of it.

- To create your own light at the end of a tunnel, follow the steps at the end of this chapter and use this book as a guide to help you along the journey.

ACKNOWLEDGMENTS

First and foremost, I would like to acknowledge the many patients I have had the privilege of working with over the years. Your courage in wanting more and your willingness to do the work necessary to pursue your right to thrive have been the inspiration and guidance for every word written here. Without you this book would not exist. To those of you who participated in the Future Directed Therapy courses where this book was developed, your honesty and feedback were invaluable. Because of you, what was first only a thought in my mind has evolved into something bigger than I could ever have conceived it to be. Watching you grow was the motivation I used to bring this book to completion and the most rewarding experience of my career. It is my greatest hope that many more will benefit from all that I have learned from you.

I would also like to thank the psychologists in training who helped coordinate the Future Directed Therapy courses — Marissa Burgoyne, Deepika Chopra, Joy Chudzynski, Chanel Kealoha, Narineh Hartoonian, Allycin Powell-Hicks, Sarah Ormseth, and Sally Chung. Your enthusiasm and passion were inspiring and your dedication something I am truly grateful for. I am very proud to know you are the future of the field of psychology. I would additionally like to thank the undergraduate volunteers Sabrina Young, Josefine Borrmann, Emily Smith, and Michelle Maile who gave not just their time but truly their hearts and their very bright minds to this project.

I owe a considerable amount of gratitude to my colleagues Robert Chernoff, PhD, whose sharp mind and honest feedback challenged me to be better; Waguih W. IsHak, MD, whose positive energy and endless encouragement always helped me to believe that it could be done; and Mark H. Rapaport, MD, whose guidance and support made everything possible.

To the editors Lisa Fugard, Anne Barthel, Jason Gardner, and Mimi Kusch, thank you kindly for the positive energy and care that you brought to this book. I feel blessed to have found such lovely human beings to share in the creation of this work. And a special thank you to Jonathan Wichmann and Jennifer Listug for rescuing this book from the slush pile.

Last, but certainly not least, I thank my friends and family who supported me through the several years it took to complete this project. I am sincerely grateful for all the kindness, understanding, and opportunities you provided that allowed me to succeed.

NOTES

AN INTRODUCTION TO FUTURE DIRECTED THERAPY

1. N. Makris, J. Biederman, M. C. Monuteaus, and L.J. Seidman, "Towards Conceptualizing a Neural Systems-Based Anatomy of Attention-Deficit/Hyperactivity Disorder," *Developmental Neuroscience* 31 (2009): 36–49.

2. E. Diener, ed., *The Science of Well-Being* (New York: Springer, 2009).

3. G. Hasler, "Can the Neuroeconomics Revolution Revolutionize Psychiatry?" *Neuroscience and Behavioral Reviews* 36 (2012): 64–78.

4. E. Nestler and W. Carlezon, "The Mesolimbic Dopamine Reward Circuit in Depression," *Biological Psychiatry* 59 (2006): 1151–59; S. Grob et al., "Dopamine-Related Deficit in Reward Learning after Catecholamine Depletion in Unmedicated, Remitted Subjects with Bulimia Nervosa," *Neuropsychopharmacology* 37 (2012): 1945–52.

5. M. Treadway and D. Zald, "Reconsidering Anhedonia in Depression: Lessons from Translational Neuroscience," *Neuroscience and Biobehavioral Reviews* 35, no. 3 (2011): 537–55.

6. M. Treadway et al., "Worth the 'EEfRT'? The Effort Expenditure for Rewards Task as an Objective Measure of Motivation and Anhedonia," *PLOS ONE* 4, no. 8 (2009), doi:10.1371/journal.pone.0006598; J. Salamone and M. Correa, "Dopamine/Adenosine Interactions Involved in Effort-Related Aspects of Food Motivation," *Appetite* 53 (2009): 422–25.

7. Treadway and Zald, "Reconsidering Anhedonia in Depression," 537–55.

8. G. Siegle, F. Ghinassi, and M. Thase, "Neurobehavioral Therapies in the 21st Century: Summary of an Emerging Field and an Extended Example of Cognitive Control Training for Depression," *Cognitive Therapy and Research* 31, no. 2 (2007): 235–62.

9. J. M. Schwartz, *The Mind and the Brain: Neuroplasticity and the Power of Mental Force* (New York: HarperCollins, 2002).

10. N. Jokic-Begic, "Cognitive-Behavioral Therapy and Neuroscience: Towards Closer Integration," *Psychological Topics* 19, no. 2 (2010): 235–54; M. Merzenich et al., "Cortical Plasticity

Underlying Perceptual, Motor, and Cognitive Skill Development: Implications for Neuro-rehabilitation," *Cold Spring Harbor Symposia on Quantitative Biology* 61 (1996): 1–8.

Chapter 1. A New Beginning

1. A. Reading, *Hope and Despair: How Perspectives of the Future Shape Human Behavior* (Baltimore: Johns Hopkins Univ. Press, 2004).
2. E. Diener, "Subjective Well-Being," *Psychological Bulletin* 95, no. 3 (1984): 542–75; A. MacLeod and C. Conway, "Well-Being and the Anticipation of Future Positive Experiences: The Role of Income, Social Networks, and Planning Ability," *Cognition and Emotion* 19, no. 3 (2005): 357–74; P. Schmuck and K. Sheldon, eds., *Life Goals and Well-Being: Towards a Positive Psychology of Human Striving* (Berlin: Hogrefe & Huber, 2001).
3. A. MacLeod et al., "Personality Disorder and Future-Directed Thinking in Parasuicide," *Journal of Personality Disorders* 18, no. 5 (2004): 459–66; R. A. Emmons, "Abstract versus Concrete Goals: Personal Striving Level, Physical Illness, and Psychological Well-Being," *Journal of Personality and Social Psychology* 62, no. 2 (1992): 292–300.
4. J. W. Atkinson, "Motivational Determinants of Risk-Taking Behavior," *Psychological Review* 64, no. 6, pt. 1 (1957): 359–72; R. S. Wyer Jr., "Effects of Task Reinforcement, Social Reinforcement, and Task Difficulty on Perseverance in Achievement-Related Activity," *Journal of Personality and Social Psychology* 8, no. 3 (1968): 269–76; M. Marshall and J. Brown, "Expectations and Realizations: The Role of Expectancies in Achievement Settings," *Motivation and Emotion* 28, no. 4 (2004): 347–61.
5. C. S. Carver and M. F. Scheier, "Origins and Functions of Positive and Negative Affect: A Control-Process View," *Psychological Review* 97, no. 1 (1990): 19–35; K. M. Sheldon et al., "Personal Goals and Psychological Growth: Testing an Intervention to Enhance Goal Attainment and Personality Integration," *Journal of Personality* 70, no. 1 (2002): 5–31; G. Lowenstein et al., "Risk as Feelings," *Psychological Bulletin* 127, no. 2 (2001): 267–86.

Chapter 2. The Value of Your Thoughts

1. E. Klinger, and W. M. Cox, "Dimensions of Thought Flow in Everyday Life," *Imagination, Cognition and Personality* 7, no. 2 (1987–1988): 105–28.
2. D. Kahneman, *Attention and Effort*, Prentice-Hall Series in Experimental Psychology (Englewood Cliffs, NJ: Prentice-Hall, 1973).
3. C. Chabris and D. Simons, *The Invisible Gorilla* (New York: Crown, 2010).
4. M. Corbetta et al., "Attentional Modulation of Neural Processing of Shape, Color, and Velocity in Humans," *Science* 248, no. 4962 (1990): 1556–59; P. Bentley et al., "Effects of Attention and Emotion on Repetition Priming and Their Modulation by Cholinergic Enhancement," *Journal of Neurophysiology* 90, no. 2 (2003): 1171–81.
5. P. Fries et al., "The Effects of Visual Stimulation and Selective Visual Attention on Rhythmic Neuronal Synchronization in Macaque Area V4," *Journal of Neuroscience* 28, no. 18 (2008): 4823–35; G. M. Edelman and G. Tononi, *A Universe of Consciousness: How Matter Becomes Imagination* (New York: Basic Books, 2000); R. Desimone, "Visual Attention

Mediated by Biased Competition in Extrastriate Visual Cortex," *Philosophical Transactions of the Royal Society B: Biological Sciences* 353, no. 1373 (1998): 1245–55.

6. J. M. Schwartz, *The Mind and the Brain: Neuroplasticity and the Power of Mental Force* (New York: HarperCollins, 2002).

7. N. Kanwisher and P. Downing, "Separating the Wheat from the Chaff," *Science* 282, no. 5386 (1998): 57–58.

8. J. Hawkins, *On Intelligence* (New York: Henry Holt, 2004).

9. K. H. Pribram and D. McGuinness, "Arousal, Activation, and Effort in the Control of Attention," *Psychological Review* 82, no. 2 (1975): 116–49.

CHAPTER 3. COMPONENTS OF THE HUMAN EXPERIENCE

1. M. Bar, *Predictions in the Brain* (New York: Oxford Univ. Press, 2011).

2. R. Nijhawan, "Visual Prediction: Psychophysics and Neurophysiology of Compensation for Time Delays," *Behavior and Brain Science* 31, no. 2 (2008): 179–98.

3. G. Hasler, "Can the Neuroeconomics Revolution Revolutionize Psychiatry?" *Neuroscience and Behavioral Reviews* 36 (2012): 64–78.

CHAPTER 4. CREATING NEW EXPECTATIONS

1. C. Soon et al., "Unconscious Determinants of Free Decisions in the Human Brain," *Nature Neuroscience* 11 (2008): 543–45.

CHAPTER 7. KNOWING WHAT YOU VALUE

1. L. Kahle, *Social Values and Social Change: Adaptation to Life in America* (New York: Praeger, 1983).

CHAPTER 9. VISUALIZING YOUR FUTURE

1. A. A. Sheikh and E. R. Korn, eds., *Imagery in Sports and Physical Performance* (Amityville, NY: Baywood Publishing, 1994).

2. E. B. Goldstein, *Sensation and Perception,* 8th ed. (Belmont, CA: Wadsworth Cengage Learning, 2009).

3. C. Soon et al., "Unconscious Determinants of Free Decisions in the Human Brain," *Nature Neuroscience* 11 (2008): 543–45.

4. D. Kahneman, *Attention and Effort,* Prentice-Hall Series in Experimental Psychology (Englewood Cliffs, NJ: Prentice-Hall, 1973); D. Kahneman and R. H. Thaler, "Anomalies: Utility Maximization and Experienced Utility," *Journal of Economic Perspectives* 20, no. 1 (2006): 221–34.

5. M. Corbetta et al., "Attentional Modulation of Neural Processing of Shape, Color, and Velocity in Humans," *Science* 248, no. 4962 (1990): 1556–59; P. Bentley et al., "Effects of Attention and Emotion on Repetition Priming and Their Modulation by Cholinergic Enhancement," *Journal of Neurophysiology* 90, no. 2 (2003): 1171–81.

6. K. Shimo et al., "Visualization of Painful Experiences Believed to Trigger the Activation of

Affective and Emotional Brain Regions in Subjects with Low Back Pain," *PLOS ONE* 11, no. 6 (2011), doi:10.1371/journal.pone.0026681; C. Berna, I. Tracey, and E. Holmes, "How a Better Understanding of Spontaneous Mental Imagery Linked to Pain Could Enhance Imagery-Based Therapy in Chronic Pain," *Journal of Experimental Psychopathology* 3, no. 2 (2012): 258–73.

7. E. A. Holmes et al., "Positive Interpretation Training: Effects of Mental Imagery versus Verbal Training on Positive Mood," in "Interpretive Biases and Ruminative Thought: Experimental Evidence and Clinical Implications," special issue, *Behavior Therapy* 37, no. 3 (2006): 237–47.

CHAPTER 10. GENERATING SOLUTIONS FOR SUCCESS

1. M. Gladwell, *Blink* (New York: Little, Brown and Company, 2005).

BIBLIOGRAPHY

Atkinson, J. W. "Motivational Determinants of Risk-Taking Behavior." *Psychological Review* 64, no. 6, pt. 1 (1957): 359–72.

Bar, M. *Predictions in the Brain*. New York: Oxford Univ. Press, 2011.

Bentley, P., P. Vuilleumier, C. M. Thiel, J. Driver, and R. J. Dolan. "Effects of Attention and Emotion on Repetition Priming and Their Modulation by Cholinergic Enhancement." *Journal of Neurophysiology* 90, no. 2 (2003): 1171–81.

Berna, C., I. Tracey, and E. Holmes. "How a Better Understanding of Spontaneous Mental Imagery Linked to Pain Could Enhance Imagery-Based Therapy in Chronic Pain." *Journal of Experimental Psychopathology* 3, no. 2 (2012): 258–73.

Carver, C. S., and M. F. Scheier. "Origins and Functions of Positive and Negative Affect: A Control-Process View." *Psychological Review* 97, no. 1 (1990): 19–35.

Chabris, C., and D. Simons. *The Invisible Gorilla*. New York: Crown, 2010.

Corbetta, M., F. M. Miezin, S. Dobmeyer, G. L. Shulman, and S. E. Petersen. "Attentional Modulation of Neural Processing of Shape, Color, and Velocity in Humans." *Science* 248, no. 4962 (1990): 1556–59.

Desimone, R. "Visual Attention Mediated by Biased Competition in Extrastriate Visual Cortex." *Philosophical Transactions of the Royal Society B: Biological Sciences* 353, no. 1373 (1998): 1245–55.

Diener, E. "Subjective Well-Being." *Psychological Bulletin* 95, no. 3 (1984): 542–75.

———, ed. *The Science of Well-Being*. New York: Springer, 2009.

Edelman, G. M., and G. Tononi. *A Universe of Consciousness: How Matter Becomes Imagination*. New York: Basic Books, 2000.

Emmons, R. A. "Abstract versus Concrete Goals: Personal Striving Level, Physical Illness, and Psychological Well-Being." *Journal of Personality and Social Psychology* 62, no. 2 (1992): 292–300.

Fries, P., T. Womelsdorf, R. Oostenveld, and R. Desimone. "The Effects of Visual Stimulation and Selective Visual Attention on Rhythmic Neuronal Synchronization in Macaque Area V4." *Journal of Neuroscience* 28, no. 18 (2008): 4823–35.

Gladwell, M. *Blink.* New York: Little, Brown and Company, 2005.

Goldstein, E. B. *Sensation and Perception,* 8th ed. Belmont, CA: Wadsworth Cengage Learning, 2009.

Grob, S., D. Pizzagalli, S. Dutra, J. Stern, H. Mörgeli, G. Milos, U. Schnyder, and G. Hasler. "Dopamine-Related Deficit in Reward Learning after Catecholamine Depletion in Unmedicated, Remitted Subjects with Bulimia Nervosa." *Neuropsychopharmacology* 37 (2012): 1945–52.

Hasler, G. "Can the Neuroeconomics Revolution Revolutionize Psychiatry?" *Neuroscience and Behavioral Reviews* 36 (2012): 64–78.

Hawkins, J. *On Intelligence.* New York: Henry Holt, 2004.

Holmes, E. A., A. Mathews, T. Dalgleish, and B. Mackintosh. "Positive Interpretation Training: Effects of Mental Imagery Versus Verbal Training on Positive Mood." In "Interpretive Biases and Ruminative Thought: Experimental Evidence and Clinical Implications," special issue, *Behavior Therapy*, 37, no. 3 (2006): 237–47.

Jokic-Begic, N. "Cognitive-Behavioral Therapy and Neuroscience: Towards Closer Integration." *Psychological Topics* 19, no. 2 (2010): 235–54.

Kahle, L. *Social Values and Social Change: Adaptation to Life in America.* New York: Praeger, 1983.

Kahneman, D. *Attention and Effort.* Prentice-Hall Series in Experimental Psychology. Englewood Cliffs, NJ: Prentice-Hall, 1973.

———, and R. H. Thaler. "Anomalies: Utility Maximization and Experienced Utility." *Journal of Economic Perspectives* 20, no. 1 (2006): 221–34.

Kanwisher, N., and P. Downing. "Separating the Wheat from the Chaff." *Science* 282, no. 5386 (1998): 57–58.

Klinger, E., and W. M. Cox. "Dimensions of Thought Flow in Everyday Life." *Imagination, Cognition and Personality* 7, no. 2 (1987–1988): 105–128.

Lowenstein, G., E. Weber, C. Hsee, and N. Welch. "Risk as Feelings." *Psychological Bulletin* 127, no. 2 (2001): 267–86.

MacLeod, A., and C. Conway. "Well-Being and the Anticipation of Future Positive Experiences: The Role of Income, Social Networks, and Planning Ability." *Cognition and Emotion* 19, no. 3 (2005): 357–74.

MacLeod, A., P. Tata, P. Tyrer, U. Schmidt, K. Davidson, and S. Thompson. "Personality Disorder and Future-Directed Thinking in Parasuicide." *Journal of Personality Disorders* 18, no. 5 (2004): 459–66.

Makris, N., J. Biederman, M. C. Monuteaus, and L. J. Seidman. "Towards Conceptualizing a Neural Systems-Based Anatomy of Attention-Deficit/Hyperactivity Disorder." *Developmental Neuroscience* 31 (2009): 36–49.

Marshall, M., and J. Brown. "Expectations and Realizations: The Role of Expectancies in Achievement Settings." *Motivation and Emotion* 28, no. 4 (2004): 347–61.

Merzenich, M., B. Wright, W. Jenkins, C. Xerri, N. Byl, S. Miller, and P. Tallal. "Cortical

Plasticity Underlying Perceptual, Motor, and Cognitive Skill Development: Implications for Neurorehabilitation." *Cold Spring Harbor Symposia on Quantitative Biology* 61 (1996): 1–8.

Nestler, E., and W. Carlezon. "The Mesolimbic Dopamine Reward Circuit in Depression." *Biological Psychiatry* 59 (2006): 1151–59.

Nijhawan, R. "Visual Prediction: Psychophysics and Neurophysiology of Compensation for Time Delays." *Behavior and Brain Science* 31, no. 2 (2008): 179–98.

Pribram, K. H., and D. McGuinness. "Arousal, Activation, and Effort in the Control of Attention." *Psychological Review* 82, no. 2 (1975): 116–49.

Reading, A. *Hope and Despair: How Perspectives of the Future Shape Human Behavior.* Baltimore: Johns Hopkins Univ. Press, 2004.

Salamone, J., and M. Correa. "Dopamine/Adenosine Interactions Involved in Effort-Related Aspects of Food Motivation." *Appetite* 53 (2009): 422–25.

Schmuck, P., and K. Sheldon, eds. *Life Goals and Well-Being: Towards a Positive Psychology of Human Striving.* Berlin: Hogrefe & Huber, 2001.

Schwartz, J. M. *The Mind and the Brain: Neuroplasticity and the Power of Mental Force.* New York: HarperCollins, 2002.

Sheikh, A. A., and E. R. Korn, eds. *Imagery in Sports and Physical Performance.* Amityville, NY: Baywood, 1994.

Sheldon, K. M., T. Kasser, K. Smith, and T. Share. "Personal Goals and Psychological Growth: Testing an Intervention to Enhance Goal Attainment and Personality Integration." *Journal of Personality* 70, no. 1 (2002): 5–31.

Shimo, K., T. Ueno, J. Younger, M. Nishihara, S. Inoue, T. Ikemoto, S. Taniguchi, and T. Ushida. "Visualization of Painful Experiences Believed to Trigger the Activation of Affective and Emotional Brain Regions in Subjects with Low Back Pain." *PLOS ONE* 11, no. 6 (2011), doi:10.1371/journal.pone.0026681.

Siegle, G., F. Ghinassi, and M. Thase. "Neurobehavioral Therapies in the 21st Century: Summary of an Emerging Field and an Extended Example of Cognitive Control Training for Depression." *Cognitive Therapy and Research* 31, no. 2 (2007): 235–62.

Soon, C., M. Brass, H. Heinze, and J. Haynes. "Unconscious Determinants of Free Decisions in the Human Brain." *Nature Neuroscience* 11 (2008): 543–45.

Treadway, M., J. Buckholtz, A. Schwartzman, W. Lambert, and D. Zald. "Worth the 'EEfRT'? The Effort Expenditure for Rewards Task as an Objective Measure of Motivation and Anhedonia." *PLOS ONE* 4, no. 8 (2009), doi:10.1371/journal.pone.0006598.

Treadway, M., and D. Zald. "Reconsidering Anhedonia in Depression: Lessons from Translational Neuroscience." *Neuroscience and Biobehavioral Reviews* 35, no. 3 (2011): 537–55.

Wyer, R. S., Jr. "Effects of Task Reinforcement, Social Reinforcement, and Task Difficulty on Perseverance in Achievement-Related Activity." *Journal of Personality and Social Psychology* 8, no. 3 (1968): 269–76.

FDT Website and Worksheet Download Information

To learn more about Future Directed Therapy
or to find a trained professional who can coach you on these skills, please go to:
www.FutureDirectedTherapy.com

For your convenience, you can also find full-size (8½" X 11") copies of the
worksheets at www.FutureDirectedTherapy.com.

Use the first four digits of the ISBN code on the back of this book
as the access code.

LETTER TO PROFESSIONALS

Dear Clinical Professional,

Thank you for your interest in Future Directed Therapy. FDT was developed over a five-year period of intensive workshops with real patients seeking treatment in the Adult Outpatient Program of the Department of Psychiatry and Behavioral Neurosciences at Cedars-Sinai Medical Center in Los Angeles, California. The patients who participated in the Future Directed Therapy courses graciously provided their feedback on all aspects of the material in the book, and the final result could not have been achieved without their help. Two published studies have examined the effectiveness of FDT, and both show that when the treatment was facilitated by a trained mental health professional, the patients who participated experienced a significant reduction in symptoms of anxiety and depression as well as reported improvements in their quality of life. Please see the research page at www.FutureDirectedTherapy.com to review copies of the research articles. We continue to conduct ongoing research and welcome the interest of any professional who would like to collaborate in conducting research using Future Directed Therapy.

While *Think Forward to Thrive* is the product of the manual used by patients who have participated in the research studies, it is important to note that this is *not* the clinician manual for Future Directed Therapy. We do not expect clinicians to be able to provide the treatment without the same extensive training and information that the professionals who participated in the studies received. The skills in *Think Forward to Thrive* may serve as tools to be added to other forms of psychotherapeutic treatment, but any professional using this book without training in FDT should not refer to the book as the sole source for providing Future Directed Therapy as an independent treatment. The clinician manual and training tools for professionals are currently in development. Please check the website www.FutureDirectedTherapy.com for more details.

Again, thank you for your interest in *Think Forward to Thrive*. I hope this book is of help to you and your patients.

Sincerely,
Jennice Vilhauer, PhD

INDEX

ABOUT THE AUTHOR

Jennice Vilhauer, PhD, is a psychologist at Emory University in Atlanta, Georgia, who specializes in the area of future-directed thinking and developing skill-based methods by which people can learn to create positive future thought and action. Her research is focused on the integration of mindfulness and future-directed thought as mechanisms for recovery and wellness. The developer of Future Directed Therapy, she has more than twelve years of experience helping clients to create better futures, and she is responsible for training other psychologists and psychiatrists in the field of cognitive therapy.

Dr. Vilhauer is the director of Emory Healthcare's Adult Outpatient Psychotherapy Program and she is an assistant professor in the Department of Psychiatry and Behavioral Science in the School of Medicine at Emory University. She formerly served as the clinical director of the Adult Outpatient Programs as well as the director of Psychology Training in the Department of Psychiatry and Behavioral Neurosciences at Cedars-Sinai Medical Center in Los Angeles. She was also an assistant clinical professor with the Department of Psychology at the University of California, Los Angeles (UCLA). She completed her undergraduate training in psychology at UCLA and her graduate training at Fordham University, followed by postdoctoral training at Columbia University.

www.futuredirectedtherapy.com

NEW WORLD LIBRARY is dedicated to publishing books and other media that inspire and challenge us to improve the quality of our lives and the world.

We are a socially and environmentally aware company. We recognize that we have an ethical responsibility to our customers, our staff members, and our planet.

We serve our customers by creating the finest publications possible on personal growth, creativity, spirituality, wellness, and other areas of emerging importance. We serve New World Library employees with generous benefits, significant profit sharing, and constant encouragement to pursue their most expansive dreams.

As a member of the Green Press Initiative, we print an increasing number of books with soy-based ink on 100 percent postconsumer-waste recycled paper. Also, we power our offices with solar energy and contribute to non-profit organizations working to make the world a better place for us all.

Our products are available in bookstores everywhere.

www.newworldlibrary.com

At NewWorldLibrary.com you can download our catalog,
subscribe to our e-newsletter, read our blog,
and link to authors' websites, videos, and podcasts.

Find us on Facebook, follow us on Twitter, and watch us on YouTube.

Send your questions and comments our way!
You make it possible for us to do what we love to do.

Phone: 415-884-2100 or 800-972-6657
Catalog requests: Ext. 10 | Orders: Ext. 52 | Fax: 415-884-2199
escort@newworldlibrary.com

NEW WORLD LIBRARY
publishing books that change lives   14 Pamaron Way, Novato, CA 94949